TEMPI VERBALI

**Il segreto per usare i tempi verbali inglesi
come un nativo in 2 settimane
Per chi è molto impegnato**

Fluent English Publishing

Xiao, Ken
Xiao, Urison

Tempi verbali: Il segreto per usare i tempi verbali inglesi come un nativo in 2 settimane Per chi è molto impegnato

Copyright © 2019 by Ken Xiao and Urison Xiao

ISBN-13: 978-1-949916-06-5
ISBN-10: 1-949916-06-5

Contenuti

Capitolo 1: Panoramica dei tempi verbali

Hai studiato inglese per anni, eppure usi ancora i tempi sbagliati. Hai provato molti metodi ma continui a commettere errori sui tempi. Sai leggere i tempi verbali, ma quando parli o scrivi non sei sicuro di quale tempo usare.

La buona notizia è che tutto questo è normale.

Ken una volta era come te, ma ora può usare i tempi inglesi come un nativo. Urison è un madrelingua inglese. In questo libro, Ken e Urison ti insegneranno il segreto per imparare i tempi inglesi senza sforzo, automaticamente e in maniera permanente… e ti insegneranno come realizzare tutto questo in sole due settimane.

Con questo libro:

- imparerai i tempi verbali senza sforzo
- imparerai automaticamente il tempo verbale
- imparerai i tempi in maniera permanente
- imparerai i tempi in 2 settimane
- imparerai i tempi senza memorizzare le regole
- imparerai ad utilizzare i tempi come un nativo
- imparerai tanto altro

Hai studiato inglese per anni, eppure usi ancora i tempi sbagliati. La ragione è semplice: i metodi di apprendimento che hai utilizzato non erano efficaci. Cambia adesso il tuo approccio. Impara da un insegnante di inglese che è già stato nei tuoi panni e ha ottenuto i risultati che desideri anche tu. Scopri qual è il segreto e seguilo per imparare i tempi inglesi in modo rapido ed efficace e per avere risultati garantiti!

Curiosità:
Se leggiamo un libro, dopo un'ora ne ricordiamo soltanto il 50%.

Imparare i tempi inglesi è molto simile al nuoto. Devi solo tuffarti

1

e iniziare.

Useremo molti esercizi per testare i tempi verbali, proprio come i nuotatori usano gli esercizi per allenare i muscoli o una piscina per praticare le loro abilità.

Leggi gli esercizi di questo libro a voce alta, ripetutamente. Se acquisti la versione audio, ascolta e ripeti la registrazione più volte. Una volta acquisite le informazioni nel tuo subconscio, i tempi inglesi diventeranno una conoscenza automatica.

In inglese, i tempi verbali ci riferiscono il tempo degli eventi o delle azioni. In altre parole, possiamo dire quando gli eventi o le azioni sono avvenuti semplicemente osservando quale tempo viene utilizzato.

Curiosità:

Esistono 14 tempi in spagnolo, 12 in inglese, sei in tedesco, quattro in francese, tre in giapponese, due in coreano e nessuno in cinese.

Ci sono tre tempi verbali di base in inglese: presente, passato e futuro.

Ciascun tempo è ulteriormente suddiviso in quattro tipologie: Simple, continuous, perfect continuous, perfect. I 12 tempi verbali inglesi sono:

Simple Present
Present Continuous
Present Perfect Continuous
Present Perfect

Simple Past
Past Continuous
Past Perfect Continuous
Past Perfect

Simple Future
Future Continuous
Future Perfect Continuous
Future Perfect

Capitolo 2: Presente

Rivediamo i tempi presenti:
Simple present
Present Continuous
Present Perfect Continuous
Present perfect

2.1 Simple Present

I **study** every day.

Questa è una cosa che faccio tutti i giorni. Succede nel presente.

They sometimes **study** together.

Loro studiano insieme – ma solo a volte. Ripetono questo processo solo una volta ogni tanto, ma ripetono questo processo nel tempo presente. Queste due frasi sono in simple present.

Usiamo il simple present:

1. Per esprimere fatti e verità generali:
   * Planets **revolve** around stars.
   * One plus one **equals** two.
   * Most birds **fly**.
   * The sun **rises** in the east.

2. Per parlare di azioni ripetute o di routine:
   * We **walk** to school every day.
   * They **study** together every Friday.
   * Sandra **takes** the bus to work.
   * Jason **gazes** at the stars at night.

3. Per parlare di abitudini:

- Andrea **drinks** milk for breakfast.
- They **shop** for groceries once a week.
- I **plant** sunflowers every April.
- Birds **eat** my sunflower seeds every August.

4. Per parlare di accordi fissi:
- The package **comes** tomorrow.
- The CEO **visits** the store on Tuesday.
- School **begins** on September 2nd.
- The library **opens** at 10.

5. Per rendere gli eventi passati più recenti:
- Trump **meets** the North Korean leader in Vietnam.
- Firefighters **rescue** a student from a burning building..
- Martin Luther King **launches** a marching campaign.
- George Washington **leads** the continental army.

6. Per dare istruzioni e indicazioni:
- **Take** I-405 and then **take** exit 5.
- **Open** the book and then **drink** some water.
- **Remove** the top cap. Then **remove** the bottom cap.
- **Boil** water. Then **add** some salt.

Nelle istruzioni e nelle indicazioni, il soggetto è "you".
- You take I-405 and then you take exit 5.
- You open the book and then you drink some water.

Diamo un'occhiata a questa frase.

We **land** on the moon.

Il verbo, **land**, è nella sua forma originale. Ora, se cambiamo il soggetto in "she," avremo bisogno di modificare il verbo.

She **lands** on the moon.

Vedi la *s* aggiunta alla fine del verbo? Quando il soggetto è la terza persona singolare, aggiungiamo una *s* alla fine del verbo. Leggi e ripeti quanto segue ad alta voce.

We land on the moon.
You land on the moon.
They land on the moon.
She lands on the moon.
He lands on the moon.
It lands on the moon.
Andrea lands on the moon.
Urison lands on the moon.
Andrea and Urison land on the moon.
My cat lands on the moon.

Ora guarda qui:

I study English.
You study English.
Andrea and Nathan study English together.

Perché non aggiungiamo una *s* alla fine di "study" in quelle frasi? I study English. Sono una persona sola. Questo perché "I" è la prima persona. Aggiungiamo una *s* solo alla terza persona singolare: He, she, it.

Scaldiamoci un po'.
I listen to audiobooks every day.
You listen to audiobooks every day.
We listen to audiobooks every day.
They listen to audiobooks every day.
He listens to audiobooks every day.
She listens to audiobooks every day.
It listens to audiobooks every day.
Andrea listens to audiobooks every day.
Urison listens to audiobooks every day.
Andrea and Urison listen to audiobooks every day.
My cat listens to audiobooks every day.

L'unico modo per imparare a nuotare è entrare in acqua e nuotare, quindi tuffiamoci.

I **breathe** every day.
You **breathe** every day.
We **breathe** every day.
They **breathe** every day.
He **breathes** every day.
She **breathes** every day.
It **breathes** every day.
Andrea **breathes** every day.
Urison **breathes** every day.
Andrea and Urison **breathe** every day.
My cat **breathes** every day.

I **wake up** at seven every day.
You **wake up** at seven every day.
We **wake up** at seven every day.
They **wake up** at seven every day.
He **wakes up** at seven every day.
She **wakes up** at seven every day.
It **wakes up** at seven every day.
Andrea **wakes up** at seven every day.
Urison **wakes up** at seven every day.
Andrea and Urison **wake up** at seven every day.
My cat **wakes up** at seven every day.

Ora un altro.

I **play** every day.
You **play** every day.
We **play** every day.
They **play** every day.
He **plays** every day.
She **plays** every day.
It **plays** every day.
Andrea **plays** every day.
Urison **plays** every day.
Andrea and Urison **play** every day.
My cat **plays** every day.

Hai notato che il verbo, play, termina con la lettera y? Qui ci sono altri esercizi:

I **enjoy** life every day.
You **enjoy** life every day.
We **enjoy** life every day.
They **enjoy** life every day.
He **enjoy** life every day.
She **enjoy** life every day.
It **enjoy** life every day.
Andrea **enjoy** life every day.
Urison **enjoy** life every day.
Andrea and Urison **enjoy** life every day.
My cat **enjoy** life every day.

I **survey** every day.
You **survey** every day.
We **survey** every day.
They **survey** every day.
He **surveys** every day.
She **surveys** every day.
It **surveys** every day.
Andrea **surveys** every day.
Urison **surveys** every day.
Andrea and Urison **survey** every day.
My cat **surveys** every day.

Ora guarda queste molto attentamente.

I **study** every day.
You **study** every day.
We **study** every day.
They **study** every day.
He **studies** every day.
She **studies** every day.
It **studies** every day.
Andrea **studies** every day.
Urison **studies** every day.

Andrea and Urison **study** every day.
My cat **studies** every day.

Perché la risposta corretta è "Andrea **studies** every day" e non "Andrea studys every day?"

Negli esercizi precedenti, abbiamo formato le forme singolari di seconda e terza persona semplicemente aggiungendo una *s* alla fine del verbo:
- Andrea **listens** to audiobooks every day.
- Andrea **breathes** every day.
- Andrea **wakes up** at seven every day.

Quindi, perché non possiamo semplicemente aggiungere una *s* alla fine di "study?"

Motivo 1:
study termina con la lettera *y*.

Ma abbiamo visto in precedenza casi che terminavano in *y* e risultavano corretti con l'aggiunta della sola *s*:
- Andrea **plays** every day.
- Andrea **enjoys** life every day.
- Andrea **surveys** every day.

"Play, enjoy, e survey" finiscono tutti con la lettera *y*. Perché "study" è diverso?

Motivo 2:
Nel verbo "study," la lettera prima della lettera *y* è una consonante.

Hai notato che nei verbi play, enjoy, e survey, le lettere prima della lettera *y* sono vocali?

Sì? Bene!

In inglese, le lettere conosciute come vocali sono a, e, i, o, u.
Quando una vocale è davanti alla lettera *y*, la lettera *y* diventa parte

della vocale e non ha bisogno di essere modificata.

Quando una vocale è davanti alla lettera *y*, aggiungi quindi solo una *s* alla fine del verbo.

Quando una consonante è davanti alla lettera *y*, cambia quindi la *y* in *i* e poi aggiungi *es* alla fine.

Ripetiamo quanto segue per acquisire tutto questo nel nostro subconscio:

I **stay** home every day.
You **stay** home every day.
We **stay** home every day.
They **stay** home every day.
He **stays** home every day.
She **stays** home every day.
It **stays** home every day.
Andrea **stays** home every day.
Urison **stays** home every day.
Andrea and Urison **stay** home every day.
My cat **stays** home every day.

I **buy** lunch every day.
You **buy** lunch every day.
We **buy** lunch every day.
They **buy** lunch every day.
He **buys** lunch every day.
She **buys** lunch every day.
It **buys** lunch every day.
Andrea **buys** lunch every day.
Urison **buys** lunch every day.
Andrea and Urison **buy** lunch every day.
My cat **buys** lunch every day.

Ora la lettera y dopo una consonante.

I **party** every day.
You **party** every day.

We **party** every day.
They **party** every day.
He **parties** every day.
She **parties** every day.
It **parties** every day.
Andrea **parties** every day.
Urison **parties** every day.
Andrea and Urison **party** every day.
My cat **parties** every day.

I **fly** every day.
You **fly** every day.
We **fly** every day.
They **fly** every day.
He **flies** every day.
She **flies** every day.
It **flies** every day.
Andrea **flies** every day.
Urison **flies** every day.
Andrea and Urison **fly** every day.
My cat **flies** every day.

Ora guardiamo con attenzione un caso diverso:

I **teach** English.
You **teach** English.
We **teach** English.
They **teach** English.
He **teaches** English.
She **teaches** English.
It **teaches** English.
Andrea **teaches** English.
Urison **teaches** English.
Andrea and Urison **teach** English.
My cat **teaches** English.

Perché la risposta giusta è "Andrea teaches English" e non
"Andrea teachs English?"

Questo perché teach termina con *ch*. Nella terza persona singolare, quando un verbo termina con *ch*, aggiunge *es* alla fine.

Facciamo altri esercizi:

I **watch** the night sky every day.
You **watch** the night sky every day.
We **watch** the night sky every day.
They **watch** the night sky every day.
He **watches** the night sky every day.
She **watches** the night sky every day.
It **watches** the night sky every day.
Andrea **watches** the night sky every day.
Urison **watches** the night sky every day.
Andrea and Urison **watch** the night sky every day.
My cat **watches** the night sky every day.

I **munch** apples every day.
You **munch** apples every day.
We **munch** apples every day.
They **munch** apples every day.
He **munches** apples every day.
She **munches** apples every day.
It **munches** apples every day.
Andrea **munches** apples every day.
Urison **munches** apples every day.
Andrea and Urison **munch** apples every day.
My cat **munches** apples every day.

Ora prova questo:

I **wish** you well.
You **wish** you well.
We **wish** you well.
They **wish** you well.
He **wishes** you well.
She **wishes** you well.
It **wishes** you well.

Andrea **wishes** you well.
Urison **wishes** you well.
Andrea and Urison **wish** you well.
My cat **wishes** you well.

Alla terza persona singolare, quando un verbo termina con *sh*, aggiunge *es* alla fine.

I **wash** the marsh every day.
You **wash** the marsh every day.
We **wash** the marsh every day.
They **wash** the marsh every day.
He **washes** the marsh every day.
She **washes** the marsh every day.
It **washes** the marsh every day.
Andrea **washes** the marsh every day.
Urison **washes** the marsh every day.
Andrea and Urison **wash** the marsh every day.
My cat **washes** the marsh every day.

I **push** the bush every day
You **push** the bush every day.
We **push** the bush every day.
They **push** the bush every day.
He **pushes** the bush every day.
She **pushes** the bush every day.
It **pushes** the bush every day.
Andrea **pushes** the bush every day.
Urison **pushes** the bush every day.
Andrea and Urison **push** the bush every day.
My cat **pushes** the bush every day.

Ora osserva attentamente queste frasi:

I **guess** you live on Earth.
You **guess** you live on Earth.
We **guess** you live on Earth.
They **guess** you live on Earth.
He **guesses** you live on Earth.

13

She **guesses** you live on Earth.
It **guesses** you live on Earth.
Andrea **guesses** you live on Earth.
Urison **guesses** you live on Earth.
Andrea and Urison **guess** you live on Earth.
My cat **guesses** you live on Earth.

Alla terza persona singolare, quando un verbo termina con *ss*, aggiunge *es* alla fine.

I **dress up** every day.
You **dress up** every day.
We **dress up** every day.
They **dress up** every day.
He **dresses up** every day.
She **dresses up** every day.
It **dresses up** every day.
Andrea **dresses up** every day.
Urison **dresses up** every day.
Andrea and Urison **dress up** every day.
My cat **dresses up** every day.

I **cross** crossroads every day.
You **cross** crossroads every day.
We **cross** crossroads every day.
They **cross** crossroads every day.
He **crosses** crossroads every day.
She **crosses** crossroads every day.
It **crosses** crossroads every day.
Andrea **crosses** crossroads every day.
Urison **crosses** crossroads every day.
Andrea and Urison **cross** crossroads every day.
My cat **crosses** crossroads every day.

Ora uno diverso:

I **buzz** along the runway.
You **buzz** along the runway.
We **buzz** along the runway.

They **buzz** along the runway.
He **buzzes** along the runway.
She **buzzes** along the runway.
It **buzzes** along the runway.
Andrea **buzzes** along the runway.
Urison **buzzes** along the runway.
Andrea and Urison **buzz** along the runway.
My cat **buzzes** along the runway.

Alla terza persona singolare, quando un verbo termina con zz, aggiunge *es* alla fine.

I **jazz** every day.
You **jazz** every day.
We **jazz** every day.
They **jazz** every day.
He **jazzes** every day.
She **jazzes** every day.
It **jazzes** every day.
Andrea **jazzes** every day.
Urison **jazzes** every day.
Andrea and Urison **jazz** every day.
My cat **jazzes** every day.

I **whizz** past the classroom every day.
You **whizz** past this classroom every day.
We **whizz** past this classroom every day.
They **whizz** past this classroom every day.
He **whizzes** past this classroom every day.
She **whizzes** past this classroom every day.
It **whizzes** past this classroom every day.
Andrea **whizzes** past this classroom every day.
Urison **whizzes** past this classroom every day.
Andrea and Urison **whizz** past this classroom every day.
My cat **whizzes** past this classroom every day.

Ora uno diverso:

I **box** my boxes for vacation.

You **box** my boxes for vacation.
We **box** my boxes for vacation.
They **box** my boxes for vacation.
He **boxes** my boxes for vacation.
She **boxes** my boxes for vacation.
It **boxes** my boxes for vacation.
Andrea **boxes** my boxes for vacation.
Urison **boxes** my boxes for vacation.
Andrea and Urison **box** my boxes for vacation.
My cat **boxes** my boxes for vacation.

Alla terza persona singolare, quando un verbo termina con *x*, aggiunge *es* alla fine.

I **relax** on my relaxation bench every day.
You **relax** on my relaxation bench every day.
We **relax** on my relaxation bench every day.
They **relax** on my relaxation bench every day.
He **relaxes** on my relaxation bench every day.
She **relaxes** on my relaxation bench every day.
It **relaxes** on my relaxation bench every day.
Andrea **relaxes** on my relaxation bench every day.
Urison **relaxes** on my relaxation bench every day.
Andrea and Urison **relax** on my relaxation bench every day.
My cat **relaxes** on my relaxation bench every day.

I **fix** my friend's car once a while.
You **fix** my friend's car once a while.
We **fix** my friend's car once a while.
They **fix** my friend's car once a while.
He **fixes** my friend's car once a while.
She **fixes** my friend's car once a while.
It **fixes** my friend's car once a while.
Andrea **fixes** my friend's car once a while.
Urison **fixes** my friend's car once a while.
Andrea and Urison **fix** my friend's car once a while.
My cat **fixes** my friend's car once a while.

Ora osserva attentamente queste frasi:

I **do** my work every day.
You **do** your work every day.
We **do** our work every day.
They **do** their work every day.
He **does** his work every day.
She **does** her work every day.
It **does** its work every day.
Andrea **does** her work every day.
Urison **does** his work every day.
Andrea and Urison **do** their work every day.
My cat **does** its work every day.

Alla terza persona singolare, quando un verbo termina con *o*, aggiunge *es* alla fine.

I **go** to work every day.
You **go** to work every day.
We **go** to work every day.
They **go** to work every day.
He **goes** to work every day.
She **goes** to work every day.
It **goes** to work every day.
Andrea **goes** to work every day.
Urison **goes** to work every day.
Andrea and Urison **go** to work every day.
My cat **goes** to work every day.

Ora qualcosa di molto diverso:

I **have** fun every day.
You **have** fun every day.
We **have** fun every day.
They **have** fun every day.
He **has** fun every day.
She **has** fun every day.
It **has** fun every day.
Andrea **has** fun every day.
Urison **has** fun every day.

Andrea and Urison **have** fun every day.
My cat **has** fun every day.

Have è un verbo irregolare. La buona notizia è che, per il tempo presente, have è l'unico che cambia in has.

I **have** water every day.
You **have** water every day.
We **have** water every day.
They **have** water every day.
He **has** water every day.
She **has** water every day.
It **has** water every day.
Andrea **has** water every day.
Urison **has** water every day.
Andrea and Urison **have** water every day.
My cat **has** water every day.

I **have** vegetables for dinner every day.
You **have** vegetables for dinner every day.
We **have** vegetables for dinner every day.
They **have** vegetables for dinner every day.
He **has** vegetables for dinner every day.
She **has** vegetables for dinner every day.
It **has** vegetables for dinner every day.
Andrea **has** vegetables for dinner every day.
Urison **has** vegetables for dinner every day.
Andrea and Urison **have** vegetables for dinner every day.
My cat **has** vegetables for dinner every day.

Qualche altro esercizio sugli irregolari:

I **am** here.
You **are** awesome.
We **are** human.
They **are** perfect.
He **is** a student.
Toronto **is** in Canada.

Computers **are** made with alien technologies.

Nelle frasi precedenti, i verbi (am, is, and are) sono chiamati *linking verbs*, o verbi copulativi. Essi non hanno azione. Non puoi solo "am". Non puoi solo "are". Questi verbi copulativi sono necessari in queste frasi. Non puoi dire soltanto I here, you awesome, he a student. I verbi collegano il soggetto alle informazioni relative al soggetto.

Congratulazioni! Abbiamo finito il simple present tense. Festeggiamo esercitandoci ancora un po':

I **am** happy.
You **are** right.
We **are** shiny.
They **are** on Earth.
He **is** a pilot.
She **is** a nurse.
It **is** cold.
UFOs **are** real.

2.2 Present Continuous

Con il present continuous, parliamo di cose che stanno accadendo in questo momento e sono incompiute. Per esempio:

Andrea **is studying** right now.

Il soggetto è Andrea, il verbo ausiliare è is, e il verbo è study. Aggiungiamo *ing* alla fine di un verbo per dimostrare che sta accadendo proprio ora.

Usiamo il present continuous per:

1. Parlare di eventi o attività costanti:
    * We **are walking** to school.
    * They **are studying** together.
    * Jason **is gazing** at the stars.
    * The birds **are eating** my sunflower seeds.

2. Parlare di eventi futuri:
    * We **are walking** to school on Monday.
    * The doors **are opening** in 10 minutes.
    * Sandra **is visiting** on Sunday.
    * Jason **is going** to Europe in a week.

Dai un'occhiata a questa frase:

We **are landing** on the moon.

Il verbo ausiliare è *are* e il verbo principale è *land* (+*ing*). Se cambiamo il soggetto in she, allora avremo bisogno di modificare l'ausilare in *is*:

She **is landing** on the moon.

Quando il soggetto è la terza persona singolare, dobbiamo usare *is* come ausiliare. Per la prima persona singolare, il verbo ausiliare è *am*. Per tutti gli altri, usa *are*. Leggi e ripeti quanto segue.

I **am landing** on the moon.
We **are landing** on the moon.
You **are landing** on the moon.
They **are landing** on the moon.
He **is landing** on the moon.
She **is landing** on the moon.
It **is landing** on the moon.
Urison **is landing** on the moon.
Andrea **is landing** on the moon.
Urison and Andrea **are landing** on the moon.
My cat **is landing** on the moon.

I **am listening** to audiobooks right now.
You **are listening** to audiobooks right now.
We **are listening** to audiobooks right now.
They **are listening** to audiobooks right now..
He **is listening** to audiobooks right now.
She **is listening** to audiobooks right now.
It **is listening** to audiobooks right now.
Andrea **is listening** to audiobooks right now.
Urison **is listening** to audiobooks right now.
Andrea and Urison **are listening** to audiobooks right now.
My cat **is listening** to audiobooks right now.

Ricordi quanto segue in merito al tempo simple present?
- I **am** here.
- You **are** awesome.
- We **are** human.
- They **are** perfect.
- He **is** a student.
- Toronto **is** in Canada.
- Computers **are** made with alien technologies.

Nel simple present, i verbi am, is, e are, sono **linking verbs**. Essi non hanno azione. Collegano soltanto il soggetto alle informazioni sul soggetto stesso. Non ci sono verbi di azione in questi esercizi.

Tuttavia, nel present continuous, i verbi, am, is, e are, sono **verbi ausiliari**. Sono seguiti dai verbi principali con un finale in *ing*. Questi verbi sono verbi d'azione.

Tuffiamoci tra loro:

I **am playing**.
You **are playing**.
We **are playing**.
They **are playing**.
He **is playing**.
She **is playing**.
It **is playing**.
Andrea **is playing**.
Urison **is playing**.
Andrea and Urison **are playing**.
My cat **is playing**.

Hai notato che "play" termina con la lettera y? Sì? Bene.

I **am enjoying** life.
You **are enjoying** life.
We **are enjoying** life.
They **are enjoying** life.
He **is enjoying** life.
She **is enjoying** life.
It **is enjoying** life.
Andrea **is enjoying** life.
Urison **is enjoying** life.
Andrea and Urison **are enjoying** life.
My cat **is enjoying** life.

Hai notato che anche "enjoy" termina con la lettera y?

Ecco alcuni esercizi. Ripetili ad alta voce per fissarli nel tuo subconscio.

I **am surveying**.

You are surveying.
We are surveying.
They are surveying.
He is surveying.
She is surveying.
It is surveying.
Andrea is surveying.
Urison is surveying.
Andrea and Urison are surveying.
My cat is surveying.

I am studying.
You are studying.
We are studying.
They are studying.
He is studying.
She is studying.
It is studying.
Andrea is studying.
Urison is studying.
Andrea and Urison are studying.
My cat is studying.

I am partying.
You are partying.
We are partying.
They are partying.
He is partying.
She is partying.
It is partying.
Andrea is partying.
Urison is partying.
Andrea and Urison are partying.
My cat is partying.

Ora, alcuni esercizi in cui il verbo non termina con una *y*.

I am teaching English.
You are teaching English.

We **are teaching** English.
They **are teaching** English.
He **is teaching** English.
She **is teaching** English.
It **is teaching** English.
Andrea **is teaching** English.
Urison **is teaching** English.
Andrea and Urison **are teaching** English.
My cat **is teaching** English.

I **am watching** the night sky.
You **are watching** the night sky.
We **are watching** the night sky.
They **are watching** the night sky.
He **is watching** the night sky.
She **is watching** the night sky.
It **is watching** the night sky.
Andrea **is watching** the night sky.
Urison **is watching** the night sky.
Andrea and Urison **are watching** the night sky.
My cat **is watching** the night sky.

I **am munching** apples.
You **are munching** apples.
We **are munching** apples.
They **are munching** apples.
He **is munching** apples.
She **is munching** apples.
It **is munching** apples.
Andrea **is munching** apples.
Urison **is munching** apples.
Andrea and Urison **are munching** apples.
My cat **is munching** apples.

Quando il verbo è accoppiato con un verbo ausiliare, aggiungi soltanto *ing* alla fine del verbo per ogni forma:

I **am washing** the marsh.
You **are washing** the marsh.

We are washing the marsh.
They are washing the marsh.
He is washing the marsh.
She is washing the marsh.
It is washing the marsh.
Andrea is washing the marsh.
Urison is washing the marsh.
Andrea and Urison are washing the marsh.
My cat is washing the marsh.

I am pushing the bush.
You are pushing the bush.
We are pushing the bush.
They are pushing the bush.
He is pushing the bush.
She is pushing the bush.
It is pushing the bush.
Andrea is pushing the bush.
Urison is pushing the bush.
Andrea and Urison are pushing the bush.
My cat is pushing the bush.

I am guessing you live on Earth.
You are guessing you live on Earth.
We are guessing you live on Earth.
They are guessing you live on Earth.
He is guessing you live on Earth.
She is guessing you live on Earth.
It is guessing you live on Earth.
Andrea is guessing you live on Earth.
Urison is guessing you live on Earth.
Andrea and Urison are guessing you live on Earth.
My cat is guessing you live on Earth.

I am dressing up.
You are dressing up.
We are dressing up.
They are dressing up.
He is dressing up.

She **is dressing** up.
It **is dressing** up.
Andrea **is dressing** up.
Urison **is dressing** up.
Andrea and Urison **are dressing** up.
My cat **is dressing** up.

I **am crossing** crossroads.
You **are crossing** crossroads.
We **are crossing** crossroads.
They **are crossing** crossroads.
He **is crossing** crossroads.
She **is crossing** crossroads.
It **is crossing** crossroads.
Andrea **is crossing** crossroads.
Urison **is crossing** crossroads.
Andrea and Urison **are crossing** crossroads.
My cat **is crossing** crossroads.

I **am buzzing** along the runway.
You **are buzzing** along the runway.
We **are buzzing** along the runway.
They **are buzzing** along the runway.
He **is buzzing** along the runway.
She **is buzzing** along the runway.
It **is buzzing** along the runway.
Andrea **is buzzing** along the runway.
Urison **is buzzing** along the runway.
Andrea and Urison **are buzzing** along the runway.
My cat **is buzzing** along the runway.

I **am jazzing**.
You **are jazzing**.
We **are jazzing**.
They **are jazzing**.
He **is jazzing**.
She **is jazzing**.
It **is jazzing**.
Andrea **is jazzing**.

Urison **is jazzing**.
Andrea and Urison **are jazzing**.
My cat **is jazzing**.

I **am boxing** my boxes for vacation.
You **are boxing** my boxes for vacation.
We **are boxing** my boxes for vacation.
They **are boxing** my boxes for vacation.
He **is boxing** my boxes for vacation.
She **is boxing** my boxes for vacation.
It **is boxing** my boxes for vacation.
Andrea **is boxing** my boxes for vacation.
Urison **is boxing** my boxes for vacation.
Andrea and Urison **are boxing** my boxes for vacation.
My cat **is boxing** my boxes for vacation.

I **am doing** my work.
You **are doing** your work.
We **are doing** our work.
They **are doing** their work.
He **is doing** his work.
She **is doing** her work.
It **is doing** its work.
Andrea **is doing** her work.
Urison **is doing** his work.
Andrea and Urison **are doing** their work.
My cat **is doing** its work.

I **am going** to work.
You **are going** to work.
We **are going** to work.
They **are going** to work.
He **is going** to work.
She **is going** to work.
It **is going** to work.
Andrea **is going** to work.
Urison **is going** to work.
Andrea and Urison **are going** to work.
My cat **is going** to work.

Ora, qualcosa di molto diverso:

I am having fun.
You are having fun.
We are having fun.
They are having fun.
He is having fun.
She is having fun.
It is having fun.
Andrea is having fun.
Urison is having fun.
Andrea and Urison are having fun.
My cat is having fun.

Have è un verbo irregolare. A differenza della terza persona singolare del simple present dove *have* diventa *has, have* nel present continuous si modifica in *having* per ogni soggetto.

Ecco altri esercizi:

I am having vegetables for dinner.
You are having vegetables for dinner.
We are having vegetables for dinner.
They are having vegetables for dinner.
He is having vegetables for dinner.
She is having vegetables for dinner.
It is having vegetables for dinner.
Andrea is having vegetables for dinner.
Urison is having vegetables for dinner.
Andrea and Urison are having vegetables for dinner.
My cat is having vegetables for dinner.

Per i verbi che terminano in *e*, rimuoviamo la *e* finale e aggiungiamo *ing*.

I am breathing.
You are breathing.
We are breathing.

They are breathing..
He is breathing.
She is breathing.
It is breathing.
Andrea is breathing.
Urison is breathing.
Andrea and Urison are breathing.
My cat is breathing.

I am waking up.
You are waking up.
We are waking up.
They are waking up.
He is waking up.
She is waking up.
It is waking up.
Andrea is waking up.
Urison is waking up.
Andrea and Urison are waking up.
My cat is waking up.

Ora uno diverso:

I am running.
You are running.
We are running.
They are running.
He is running.
She is running.
It is running.
Andrea is running.
Urison is running.
Andrea and Urison are running.
My cat is running.

Hai notato che il verbo, run, ora ha due *n*? Cosa succede se aggiungiamo semplicemente *ing* a run senza raddoppiare la *n*? La pronuncia cambierà.

Ecco alcuni esercizi:

I **am swimming**.
You **are swimming**.
We **are swimming**.
They **are swimming**.
He **is swimming**.
She **is swimming**.
It **is swimming**.
Andrea **is swimming**.
Urison **is swimming**.
Andrea and Urison **are swimming**.

I **am cutting**.
You **are cutting**.
We **are cutting**.
They **are cutting**.
He **is cutting**.
She **is cutting**.
It **is cutting**.
Andrea **is cutting**.
Urison **is cutting**.
Andrea and Urison **are cutting**.
My cat **is cutting**.

2.3 Present Perfect Continuous

Usiamo il present perfect continuous per azioni che sono iniziate nel passato, continuano ancora adesso e potrebbero continuare nel futuro. Ecco un esempio:

Andrea **has been studying** since morning.

Lei ha iniziato la mattina, sta ancora studiando e potrebbe continuare a studiare a lungo.

Il soggetto è Andrea e il verbo è to study. *Ing* alla fine di un verbo significa che sta accadendo proprio ora. Il verbo ausiliare, "has been," ci dice che Andrea stava studiando e continua a farlo.

Diamo un'occhiata a questa frase:

They **have been working** on the moon for three hours.

Quando il soggetto viene modificato in *they*, il verbo ausiliare cambia in *have been*.

Usiamo il present perfect continuous per parlare di eventi o attività iniziati nel passato e che continuano nel presente e nel futuro:
- We **have been walking** to school for 10 minutes.
- They **have been studying** together for three hours.
- Jason **has been gazing** at the stars since eight.
- The birds **have been eating** my sunflower seeds since morning.

Ecco alcuni esercizi. Ripetili ad alta voce.

I **have been listening** to audiobooks for three hours.
You **have been listening** to audiobooks for three hours.
We **have been listening** to audiobooks for three hours.
They **have been listening** to audiobooks for three hours.
He **has been listening** to audiobooks for three hours.
She **has been listening** to audiobooks for three hours.

It has been listening to audiobooks for three hours.
Andrea has been listening to audiobooks for three hours.
Urison has been listening to audiobooks for three hours.
Andrea and Urison have been listening to audiobooks for three hours.
My cat has been listening to audiobooks for three hours.

I have been playing the piano for 30 minutes.
You have been playing the piano for 30 minutes.
We have been playing the piano for 30 minutes.
They have been playing the piano for 30 minutes.
He has been playing the piano for 30 minutes.
She has been playing the piano for 30 minutes.
It has been playing the piano for 30 minutes.
Andrea has been playing the piano for 30 minutes.
Urison has been playing the piano for 30 minutes.
Andrea and Urison have been playing the piano for 30 minutes.
My cat has been playing the piano for 30 minutes.

I have been enjoying life for a year.
You have been enjoying life for a year.
We have been enjoying life for a year.
They have been enjoying life for a year.
He has been enjoying life for a year.
She has been enjoying life for a year.
It has been enjoying life for a year.
Andrea has been enjoying life for a year.
Urison has been enjoying life for a year.
Andrea and Urison have been enjoying life for a year.
My cat has been enjoying life for a year.

I have been surveying human interactions for three months.
You have been surveying human interactions for three months.
We have been surveying human interactions for three months.
They have been surveying human interactions for three months.
He has been surveying human interactions for three months.
She has been surveying human interactions for three months.
It has been surveying human interactions for three months.
Andrea has been surveying human interactions for three months.

Urison **has been surveying** human interactions for three months.
Andrea and Urison **have been surveying** human interactions for three months.
My cat **has been surveying** human interactions for three months.

Continua ad esercitarti.

I **have been studying** since noon.
You **have been studying** since noon.
We **have been studying** since noon.
They **have been studying** since noon.
He **has been studying** since noon.
She **has been studying** since noon.
It **has been studying** since noon.
Andrea **has been studying** since noon.
Urison **has been studying** since noon.
Andrea and Urison **have been studying** since noon.
My cat **has been studying** since noon.

I **have been partying** since the party started.
You **have been partying** since the party started.
We **have been partying** since the party started.
They **have been partying** since the party started.
He **has been partying** since the party started.
She **has been partying** since the party started.
It **has been partying** since the party started.
Andrea **has been partying** since the party started.
Urison **has been partying** since the party started.
Andrea and Urison **have been partying** since the party started.
My cat **has been partying** since the party started.

Ora con il finale *ch*:

I **have been teaching** English since the opening of this school.
You **have been teaching** English since the opening of this school.
We **have been teaching** English since the opening of this school.
They **have been teaching** English since the opening of this school.
He **has been teaching** English since the opening of this school.
She **has been teaching** English since the opening of this school.

It **has been teaching** English since the opening of this school.
Andrea **has been teaching** English since the opening of this school.
Urison **has been teaching** English since the opening of this school.
Andrea and Urison **have been teaching** English since the opening of this school.
My cat **has been teaching** English since the opening of this school.

I **have been watching** the night sky for four hours.
You **have been watching** the night sky for four hours.
We **have been watching** the night sky for four hours.
They **have been watching** the night sky for four hours.
He **has been watching** the night sky for four hours.
She **has been watching** the night sky for four hours.
It **has been watching** the night sky for four hours.
Andrea **has been watching** the night sky for four hours.
Urison **has been watching** the night sky for four hours.
Andrea and Urison **have been watching** the night sky for four hours.
My cat **has been watching** the night sky for four hours.

I **have been munching** apples for three minutes.
You **have been munching** apples for three minutes.
We **have been munching** apples for three minutes.
They **have been munching** apples for three minutes.
He **has been munching** apples for three minutes.
She **has been munching** apples for three minutes.
It **has been munching** apples for three minutes.
Andrea **has been munching** apples for three minutes.
Urison **has been munching** apples for three minutes.
Andrea and Urison **have been munching** apples for three minutes.
My cat **has been munching** apples for three minutes.

Adesso con il finale *sh*:

I **have been washing** the marsh since five.
You **have been washing** the marsh since five.
We **have been washing** the marsh since five.

34

They **have been washing** the marsh since five.
He **has been washing** the marsh since five.
She **has been washing** the marsh since five.
It **has been washing** the marsh since five.
Andrea **has been washing** the marsh since five.
Urison **has been washing** the marsh since five.
Andrea and Urison **have been washing** the marsh since five.
My cat **has been washing** the marsh since five.

I **have been pushing** the bush since the beginning of the martial art training.
You **have been pushing** the bush since the beginning of the martial art training.
We **have been pushing** the bush since the beginning of the martial art training.
They **have been pushing** the bush since the beginning of the martial art training.
He **has been pushing** the bush since the beginning of the martial art training.
She **has been pushing** the bush since the beginning of the martial art training.
It **has been pushing** the bush since the beginning of the martial art training.
Andrea **has been pushing** the bush since the beginning of the martial art training.
Urison **has been pushing** the bush since the beginning of the martial art training.
Andrea and Urison **have been pushing** the bush since the beginning of the martial art training.
My cat **has been pushing** the bush since the beginning of the martial art training.

Ora con il finale *ss*:

I **have been dressing** up since the dresser was opened.
You **have been dressing** up since the dresser was opened.
We **have been dressing** up since the dresser was opened.
They **have been dressing** up since the dresser was opened.
He **has been dressing** up since the dresser was opened.

She **has been dressing** up since the dresser was opened.
It **has been dressing** up since the dresser was opened.
Andrea **has been dressing** up since the dresser was opened.
Urison **has been dressing** up since the dresser was opened.
Andrea and Urison **have been dressing** up since the dresser was opened.
My cat **has been dressing** up since the dresser was opened.

I **have been crossing** crossroads after age 11.
You **have been crossing** crossroads after age 11.
We **have been crossing** crossroads after age 11.
They **have been crossing** crossroads after age 11.
He **has been crossing** crossroads after age 11.
She **has been crossing** crossroads after age 11.
It **has been crossing** crossroads after age 11.
Andrea **has been crossing** crossroads after age 11.
Urison **has been crossing** crossroads after age 11.
Andrea and Urison **have been crossing** crossroads after age 11.
My cat **has been crossing** crossroads after age 11.

Ora con il fianle *zz*:

I **have been buzzing** along the runway all morning.
You **have been buzzing** along the runway all morning.
We **have been buzzing** along the runway all morning.
They **have been buzzing** along the runway all morning.
He **has been buzzing** along the runway all morning.
She **has been buzzing** along the runway all morning.
It **has been buzzing** along the runway all morning.
Andrea **has been buzzing** along the runway all morning.
Urison **has been buzzing** along the runway all morning.
Andrea and Urison **have been buzzing** along the runway all morning.
My cat **has been buzzing** along the runway all morning.

I **have been jazzing** all night.
You **have been jazzing** all night.
We **have been jazzing** all night.
They **have been jazzing** all night.

He **has been jazzing** all night.
She **has been jazzing** all night.
It **has been jazzing** all night.
Andrea **has been jazzing** all night.
Urison **has been jazzing** all night.
Andrea and Urison **have been jazzing** all night.
My cat **has been jazzing** all night.

Adesso con il finale *x*:

I **have been boxing** my boxes since dawn.
You **have been boxing** my boxes since dawn.
We **have been boxing** my boxes since dawn.
They **have been boxing** my boxes since dawn.
He **has been boxing** my boxes since dawn.
She **has been boxing** my boxes since dawn.
It **has been boxing** my boxes since dawn.
Andrea **has been boxing** my boxes since dawn.
Urison **has been boxing** my boxes since dawn.
Andrea and Urison **have been boxing** my boxes since dawn.
My cat **has been boxing** my boxes since dawn.

Ora con il finale *o*:

I **have been doing** my work all day.
You **have been doing** your work all day.
We **have been doing** our work all day.
They **have been doing** their work all day.
He **has been doing** his work all day.
She **has been doing** her work all day.
It **has been doing** its work all day.
Andrea **has been doing** her work all day.
Urison **has been doing** his work all day.
Andrea and Urison **have been doing** their work all day.
My cat **has been doing** its work all day.

I **have been going** around all day.
You **have been going** around all day.
We **have been going** around all day.

They **have been going** around all day.
He **has been going** around all day.
She **has been going** around all day.
It **has been going** around all day.
Andrea **has been going** around all day.
Urison **has been going** around all day.
Andrea and Urison **have been going** around all day.
My cat **has been going** around all day.

Ora prova questo:

I **have been having** fun since the party started.
You **have been having** fun since the party started.
We **have been having** fun since the party started.
They **have been having** fun since the party started.
He **has been having** fun since the party started.
She **has been having** fun since the party started.
It **has been having** fun since the party started.
Andrea **has been having** fun since the party started.
Urison **has been having** fun since the party started.
Andrea and Urison **have been having** fun since the party started.
My cat **has been having** fun since the party started.

"Have been" e "has been" sono frasi ausiliari. Have è il verbo principale.

I **have been having** vegetables for dinner for three years.
You **have been having** vegetables for dinner for three years.
We **have been having** vegetables for dinner for three years.
They **have been having** vegetables for dinner for three years.
He **has been having** vegetables for dinner for three years.
She **has been having** vegetables for dinner for three years.
It **has been having** vegetables for dinner for three years.
Andrea **has been having** vegetables for dinner for three years.
Urison **has been having** vegetables for dinner for three years.
Andrea and Urison **have been having** vegetables for dinner for three years.
My cat **has been having** vegetables for dinner for three years.

Ora con il finale *th*:

I **have been breathing** since birth.
You **have been breathing** since birth.
We **have been breathing** since birth.
They **have been breathing** since birth..
He **has been breathing** since birth.
She **has been breathing** since birth.
It **has been breathing** since birth.
Andrea **has been breathing** since birth.
Urison **has been breathing** since birth.
Andrea and Urison **have been breathing** since birth.
My cat **has been breathing** since birth.

E ora i verbi monosillabici:

I **have been running** for an hour.
You **have been running** for an hour.
We **have been running** for an hour.
They **have been running** for an hour.
He **has been running** for an hour.
She **has been running** for an hour.
It **has been running** for an hour.
Andrea **has been running** for an hour.
Urison **has been running** for an hour.
Andrea and Urison **have been running** for an hour.
My cat **has been running** for an hour.

I **have been swimming** after the water was tested.
You **have been swimming** after the water was tested.
We **have been swimming** after the water was tested.
They **have been swimming** after the water was tested.
He **has been swimming** after the water was tested.
She **has been swimming** after the water was tested.
It **has been swimming** after the water was tested.
Andrea **has been swimming** after the water was tested.
Urison **has been swimming** after the water was tested.
Andrea and Urison **have been swimming** after the water was tested.

My cat **has been swimming** after the water was tested.

2.4 Present Perfect

Osserva questi due esempi:

Andrea **has been studying** music for five years.
Andrea **has studied** music for five years.

Nel primo esempio, Andrea ha studiato musica ma non ha ancora finito. Andrea può continuare a studiare musica in futuro. Questo è il present perfect continuous. Nel secondo esempio, Andrea ha studiato e continua a studiare. Questo è il present perfect.

Questi due, sebbene siano tempi diversi, hanno lo stesso significato. Possiamo usare uno qualsiasi di loro per dire la stessa cosa. Diamo comunque un'occhiata ai seguenti esempi.

Andrea **has been learning** this piece of music.
Andrea **has learned** this piece of music.

Questi due esempi, tuttavia, hanno due significati completamente diversi. Nel primo caso, Andrea ha imparato questo brano musicale e continua a imparare lo stesso brano. Questo è il present perfect continuous. Nel secondo caso, Andrea ha già imparato questo brano e si è fermata. Se lo desidera, può continuare a imparare questo brano in un secondo momento, ma per ora questa azione è finita. Questo è il present perfect.

Con il present perfect, parliamo di azioni che sono accadute in passato, che continuano nel presente e che possono proseguire nel futuro. Ecco un esempio:

Andrea **has studied** music for five years.

Il soggetto è *Andrea*, il verbo ausiliare è *has*, e il verbo è *study* al participio passato.

Usiamo il present perfect tense per:

1. Parlare di cose accadute nel passato e che continuano nel presente:
- Andrea **has studied** music for five years.
- They **have studied** together for two years.
- Jason **has gazed** at the stars for an hour.
- The birds **have eaten** my sunflower seeds for three days.

2. Parlare di azioni che non sono ancora finite:
- Andrea **has studied** hard this year.
- They **have studied** together these two years.
- Jason **has gazed** at the stars this hour.
- The birds **have eaten** my sunflower seeds these days.

3. Parlare di azioni ripetute in un periodo non specificato tra il passato e il presente:
- Andrea **has studied** that piece of music six times.
- They **have studied** together many times.
- Jason **has gazed** at the stars frequently.
- The birds **have eaten** my sunflower seeds many times already.

4. Parlare di azioni che sono state appena completate:
- Andrea **has** just **finished** studying.
- They **have** just **finished**.
- Jason **has** just **gazed** at the stars.
- The birds **have** just **eaten** my sunflower seeds.

5. Parlare di azioni il cui tempo non è importante
- Andrea **has studied** violin, viola, and cello.
- They **have been** to Grand Canyon.
- Jason **has seen** that movie.
- The birds **have eaten** my sunflower seeds.

Per prima cosa osserva questi esempi:

They **have worked** on the moon for 30 minutes.

Questa è una frase standard al present perfect. Il soggetto è *they*, il verbo ausiliare è have, e il verbo principale è *work* alla sua forma al participio passato.

Cos'è il participio passato? Osserva il seguente schema:

Verbo	Participio passato
act	acted
be	been
begin	begun

Per i verbi regolari, aggiungiamo *ed* alla fine del verbo. Per i verbi irregolari, usiamo la rispettiva forma del participio passato.

Ecco una lista di verbi irregolari comuni.

Verbo	Tempo Passato	Participio Passato
arise	arose	arisen
be	was/were	been
bear	bore	borne
become	became	become
begin	began	begun
bite	bit	bitten
blow	blew	blown
break	broke	broken
bring	brought	brought
buy	bought	bought
catch	caught	caught
choose	chose	chosen
come	came	come

creep	crept	crept
dive	dove	dived
do	did	done
draw	drew	drawn
drink	drank	drunk
drive	drove	driven
eat	ate	eaten
fall	fell	fallen
fight	fought	fought
fly	flew	flown
forget	forgot	forgotten
forgive	forgave	forgiven
freeze	froze	frozen
get	got	got/gotten
give	gave	given
go	went	gone
grow	grew	grown
hang	hung	hung
have	had	had
hide	hid	hidden
know	knew	known
lay	laid	laid
lead	led	led
lie	lay	lain
light	lit	lit
lose	lost	lost
prove	proved	proven
ride	rode	ridden
ring	rang	rung
rise	rose	risen
run	ran	run
see	saw	seen
seek	sought	sought
set	set	set
shake	shook	shaken
sing	sang	sung
sink	sank	sunk

sit	sat	sat
speak	spoke	spoken
spring	sprung	sprung
steal	stole	stolen
sting	stung	stung
strike	struck	struck
swear	swore	sworn
swim	swam	swum
swing	swung	swung
take	took	taken
tear	tore	torn
throw	threw	thrown
wake	woke	woken
wear	wore	worn
write	wrote	written

Tuffiamoci in questi esercizi:

I **have thrown** a rock into the water.
You **have thrown** a rock into the water.
We **have thrown** a rock into the water.
They **have thrown** a rock into the water.
He **has thrown** a rock into the water.
She **has thrown** a rock into the water.
It **has thrown** a rock into the water.
Andrea **has thrown** a rock into the water.
Urison **has thrown** a rock into the water.
Andrea and Urison **have thrown** a rock into the water.
My cat **has thrown** a rock into the water.

Affrontiamo questo esercizio. "A rock." *A* indica che ho lanciato un sasso qualunque nell'acqua e posso continuare a lanciare sassi. Questa azione può continuare. Qui possiamo usare il present perfect, **o** il present perfect continuous.

Un altro esercizio:

I **have thrown** the rock into the water.
You **have thrown** the rock into the water.
We **have thrown** the rock into the water.
They **have thrown** the rock into the water.
He **has thrown** the rock into the water.
She **has thrown** the rock into the water.
It **has thrown** the rock into the water.
Andrea **has thrown** the rock into the water.
Urison **has thrown** the rock into the water.
Andrea and Urison **have thrown** the rock into the water.
My cat **has thrown** the rock into the water.

Diamo un'occhiata qui. "The rock." *The* indica che sto gettando un particolare sasso nell'acqua. Una volta che l'ho lanciato, non ci sono più sassi da gettare. Questa azione è terminata. Qui possiamo usare solo il present perfect.

Ecco altri esercizi:

I **have conveyed** the message.
You **have conveyed** the message.
We **have conveyed** the message.
They **have conveyed** the message.
He **has conveyed** the message.
She **has conveyed** the message.
It **has conveyed** the message.
Andrea **has conveyed** the message.
Urison **has conveyed** the message.
Andrea and Urison **have conveyed** the message.
My cat **has conveyed** the message.

La stessa cosa succede qui. "The message." C'è un messaggio specifico e io l'ho trasmesso. Non ci sono altri messaggi da trasmettere. Questa azione è finita. Possiamo usare solo il present perfect.

Proviamo con altre frasi:

I **have taken** my flying lesson this week.

You **have taken** your flying lesson this week.
We **have taken** our flying lesson this week.
They **have taken** their flying lesson this week.
He **has taken** his flying lesson this week.
She **has taken** her flying lesson this week.
It **has taken** its flying lesson this week.
Andrea **has taken** her flying lesson this week.
Urison **has taken** his flying lesson this week.
Andrea and Urison **have taken** their flying lesson this week.
My cat **has taken** its flying lesson this week.

I **have written** the letter.
You **have written** the letter.
We **have written** the letter.
They **have written** the letter.
He **has written** the letter.
She **has written** the letter.
It **has written** the letter.
Andrea **has written** the letter.
Urison **has written** the letter.
Andrea and Urison **have written** the letter.
My cat **has written** the letter.

I **have planted** sunflower seeds this year.
You **have planted** sunflower seeds this year.
We **have planted** sunflower seeds this year.
They **have planted** sunflower seeds this year.
He **has planted** sunflower seeds this year.
She **has planted** sunflower seeds this year.
It **has planted** sunflower seeds this year.
Andrea **has planted** sunflower seeds this year.
Urison **has planted** sunflower seeds this year.
Andrea and Urison **have planted** sunflower seeds this year.
My cat **has planted** sunflower seeds this year

Ora diamo un'occhiata a un esercizio diverso:

I **have enjoyed** life for three days.
You **have enjoyed** life for three days.

We **have enjoyed** life for three days.
They **have enjoyed** life for three days.
He **has enjoyed** life for three days.
She **has enjoyed** life for three days.
It **has enjoyed** life for three days.
Andrea **has enjoyed** life for three days.
Urison **has enjoyed** life for three days.
Andrea and Urison **have enjoyed** life for three days.
My cat **has enjoyed** life for three days.

"I **have enjoyed** life for three days." Posso continuare a godermi la vita per più tempo. Questa azione può continuare. Pertanto, possiamo scrivere questa frase anche al present perfect continuous: "I **have been enjoying** life for three days."

I **have played** the piano for a long time.
You **have played** the piano for a long time.
We **have played** the piano for a long time.
They **have played** the piano for a long time.
He **has played** the piano for a long time.
She **has played** the piano for a long time.
It **has played** the piano for a long time.
Andrea **has played** the piano for a long time.
Urison **has played** the piano for a long time.
Andrea and Urison **have played** the piano for a long time.
My cat **has played** the piano for a long time.

La stessa cosa accade in questo esercizio. Posso continuare a suonare il piano per un tempo più lungo. Questa azione può continuare. Pertanto, possiamo scrivere questa frase anche nel present perfect continuous.

Proviamo più esercizi:

I **have surveyed** human interactions for three months.
You **have surveyed** human interactions for three months.
We **have surveyed** human interactions for three months.
They **have surveyed** human interactions for three months.
He **has surveyed** human interactions for three months.

48

She **has surveyed** human interactions for three months.
It **has surveyed** human interactions for three months.
Andrea **has surveyed** human interactions for three months.
Urison **has surveyed** human interactions for three months.
Andrea and Urison **have surveyed** human interactions for three months.
My cat **has surveyed** human interactions for three months.

Continuiamo con le seguenti frasi:

I **have partied** since the party started.
You **have partied** since the party started.
We **have partied** since the party started.
They **have partied** since the party started.
He **has partied** since the party started.
She **has partied** since the party started.
It **has partied** since the party started.
Andrea **has partied** since the party started.
Urison **has partied** since the party started.
Andrea and Urison **have partied** since the party started.
My cat **has partied** since the party started.

I **have watched** the night sky for four hours.
You **have watched** the night sky for four hours.
We **have watched** the night sky for four hours.
They **have watched** the night sky for four hours.
He **has watched** the night sky for four hours.
She **has watched** the night sky for four hours.
It **has watched** the night sky for four hours.
Andrea **has watched** the night sky for four hours.
Urison **has watched** the night sky for four hours.
Andrea and Urison **have watched** the night sky for four hours.
My cat **has watched** the night sky for four hours.

I **have taught** English since the opening of this school.
You **have taught** English since the opening of this school.
We **have taught** English since the opening of this school.
They **have taught** English since the opening of this school.
He **has taught** English since the opening of this school.

She **has taught** English since the opening of this school.
It **has taught** English since the opening of this school.
Andrea **has taught** English since the opening of this school.
Urison **has taught** English since the opening of this school.
Andrea and Urison **have taught** English since the opening of this school.
My cat **has taught** English since the opening of this school.

Eccone altre:

I **have pushed** the bush since the beginning of the martial art training.
You **have pushed** the bush since the beginning of the martial art training.
We **have pushed** the bush since the beginning of the martial art training.
They **have pushed** the bush since the beginning of the martial art training.
He **has pushed** the bush since the beginning of the martial art training.
She **has pushed** the bush since the beginning of the martial art training.
It **has pushed** the bush since the beginning of the martial art training.
Andrea **has pushed** the bush since the beginning of martial art training.
Urison **has pushed** the bush since the beginning of the martial art training.
Andrea and Urison **have pushed** the bush since the beginning of the martial art training.
My cat **has pushed** the bush since the beginning of the martial art training.

I **have crossed** crossroads after age 11.
You **have crossed** crossroads after age 11.
We **have crossed** crossroads after age 11.
They **have crossed** crossroads after age 11.
He **has crossed** crossroads after age 11.
She **has crossed** crossroads after age 11.

It **has crossed** crossroads after age 11.
Andrea **has crossed** crossroads after age 11.
Urison **has crossed** crossroads after age 11.
Andrea and Urison **have crossed** crossroads after age 11.
My cat **has crossed** crossroads after age 11.

I **have buzzed** along the runway all morning.
You **have buzzed** along the runway all morning.
We **have buzzed** along the runway all morning.
They **have buzzed** along the runway all morning.
He **has buzzed** along the runway all morning.
She **has buzzed** along the runway all morning.
It **has buzzed** along the runway all morning.
Andrea **has buzzed** along the runway all morning.
Urison **has buzzed** along the runway all morning.
Andrea and Urison **have buzzed** along the runway all morning.
My cat **has buzzed** along the runway all morning.

I **have jazzed** all night.
You **have jazzed** all night.
We **have jazzed** all night.
They **have jazzed** all night.
He **has jazzed** all night.
She **has jazzed** all night.
It **has jazzed** all night.
Andrea **has jazzed** all night.
Urison **has jazzed** all night.
Andrea and Urison **have jazzed** all night.
My cat **has jazzed** all night.

I **have boxed** my boxes.
You **have boxed** my boxes.
We **have boxed** my boxes.
They **have boxed** my boxes.
He **has boxed** my boxes.
She **has boxed** my boxes.
It **has boxed** my boxes.
Andrea **has boxed** my boxes.
Urison **has boxed** my boxes.

Andrea and Urison **have boxed** my boxes.
My cat **has boxed** my boxes.

I **have done** my work.
You **have done** your work.
We **have done** our work.
They **have done** their work.
He **has done** his work.
She **has done** her work.
It **has done** its work.
Andrea **has done** her work.
Urison **has done** his work.
Andrea and Urison **have done** their work.
My cat **has done** its work.

I **have gone** all the way to the end.
You **have gone** all the way to the end.
We **have gone** all the way to the end.
They **have gone** all the way to the end.
He **has gone** all the way to the end.
She **has gone** all the way to the end.
It **has gone** all the way to the end.
Andrea **has gone** all the way to the end.
Urison **has gone** all the way to the end.
Andrea and Urison **have gone** all the way to the end.
My cat **has gone** all the way to the end.

I **have had** fun.
You **have had** fun.
We **have had** fun.
They **have had** fun.
He **has had** fun.
She **has had** fun.
It **has had** fun.
Andrea **has had** fun.
Urison **has had** fun.
Andrea and Urison **have had** fun.
My cat **has had** fun.

I **have had** vegetables.
You **have had** vegetables.
We **have had** vegetables.
They **have had** vegetables.
He **has had** vegetables.
She **has had** vegetables.
It **has had** vegetables.
Andrea **has had** vegetables.
Urison **has had** vegetables.
Andrea and Urison **have had** vegetables.
My cat **has had** vegetables.

I **have run** for an hour.
You **have run** for an hour.
We **have run** for an hour.
They **have run** for an hour.
He **has run** for an hour.
She **has run** for an hour.
It **has run** for an hour.
Andrea **has run** for an hour.
Urison **has run** for an hour.
Andrea and Urison **have run** for an hour.
My cat **has run** for an hour.

I **have swum** before the water was tested.
You **have swum** before the water was tested.
We **have swum** before the water was tested.
They **have swum** before the water was tested.
He **has swum** before the water was tested.
She **has swum** before the water was tested.
It **has swum** before the water was tested.
Andrea **has swum** before the water was tested.
Urison **has swum** before the water was tested.
Andrea and Urison **have swum** before the water was tested.
My cat **has swum** before the water was tested.

I **have washed** marsh for five years.
You **have washed** marsh for five years.
We **have washed** marsh for five years.

They **have washed** marsh for five years.
He **has washed** marsh for five years.
She **has washed** marsh for five years.
It **has washed** marsh for five years.
Andrea **has washed** marsh for five years.
Urison **has washed** marsh for five years.
Andrea and Urison **have washed** marsh for five years.
My cat **has washed** marsh for five years.

I **have studied** hard this year.
You **have studied** hard this year.
We **have studied** hard this year.
They **have studied** hard this year.
He **has studied** hard this year.
She **has studied** hard this year.
It **has studied** hard this year.
Andrea **has studied** hard this year.
Urison **has studied** hard this year.
Andrea and Urison **have studied** hard this year.
My cat **has studied** hard this year.

I **have studied** this piece of music six times.
You **have studied** this piece of music six times.
We **have studied** this piece of music six times.
They **have studied** this piece of music six times.
He **has studied** this piece of music six times.
She **has studied** this piece of music six times.
It **has studied** this piece of music six times.
Andrea **has studied** this piece of music six times.
Urison **has studied** this piece of music six times.
Andrea and Urison **have studied** this piece of music six times.
My cat **has studied** this piece of music six times.

I **have** just **finished studying**.
You **have** just **finished studying**.
We **have** just **finished studying**.
They **have** just **finished studying**.
He **has** just **finished studying**.
She **has** just **finished studying**.

It **has** just **finished studying**.
Andrea **has** just **finished studying**.
Urison **has** just **finished studying**.
Andrea and Urison **have** just **finished studying**.
My cat **has** just **finished studying**.

E adesso questo.

I **have been** to Grand Canyon.
You **have been** to Grand Canyon.
We **have been** to Grand Canyon.
They **have been** to Grand Canyon.
He **has been** to Grand Canyon.
She **has been** to Grand Canyon.
It **has been** to Grand Canyon.
Andrea **has been** to Grand Canyon.
Urison **has been** to Grand Canyon.
Andrea and Urison **have been** to Grand Canyon.
My cat **has been** to Grand Canyon.

Capitolo 3: Passato

Il tempo passato è utilizzato per descrivere azioni che sono già accadute. Potrebbero essere successe un anno fa, un giorno fa o un secondo fa.

Rivediamo. I tempi passati sono:

Simple Past
Past Continuous
Past Perfect Continuous
Past Perfect

3.1 Simple Past

Dai un'occhiata a questa frase:

We **landed** on the moon in 1969.

Il verbo, land, è al passato. Ora, se cambiamo il soggetto in *she*, non abbiamo bisogno di modificare nulla.

She **landed** on the moon in 1969.

Usiamo il simple past per parlare di cose accadute nel passato:

1. In un momento specifico:
   - Andrea **played** the piano yesterday.
   - They **studied** together last year.
   - Jason **gazed** at the stars last night.
   - Birds ate my sunflower seeds this morning.

2. In un momento non specifico:
   - Andrea **played** the piano a long time ago.
   - They **studied** together when they were five.
   - Jason **gazed** at the stars some time ago.
   - Birds ate my sunflower seeds the other day.

3. Per un periodo di tempo:
   - Andrea **played** the piano for two weeks.
   - They **studied** together for two years.
   - Jason **gazed** at the stars for three days.
   - Birds **ate** my sunflower seeds for an hour.

Iniziamo:

I **woke** up at seven this morning.
You **woke** up at seven this morning.
We **woke** up at seven this morning.
They **woke** up at seven this morning.

He **woke** up at seven this morning.
She **woke** up at seven this morning.
It **woke** up at seven this morning.
Andrea **woke** up at seven this morning.
Urison **woke** up at seven this morning.
Andrea and Urison **woke** up at seven this morning.
My cat **woke** up at seven this morning.

I **played** the piano yesterday.
You **played** the piano yesterday.
We **played** the piano yesterday.
They **played** the piano yesterday.
He **played** the piano yesterday.
She **played** the piano yesterday.
It **played** the piano yesterday.
Andrea **played** the piano yesterday.
Urison **played** the piano yesterday.
Andrea and Urison **played** the piano yesterday.
My cat **played** the piano yesterday.

I **enjoyed** the show yesterday.
You **enjoyed** the show yesterday.
We **enjoyed** the show yesterday.
They **enjoyed** the show yesterday.
He **enjoyed** the show yesterday.
She **enjoyed** the show yesterday.
It **enjoyed** the show yesterday.
Andrea **enjoyed** the show yesterday.
Urison **enjoyed** the show yesterday.
Andrea and Urison **enjoyed** the show yesterday.
My cat **enjoyed** the show yesterday.

I **threw** a rock into the water.
You **threw** a rock into the water.
We **threw** a rock into the water.
They **threw** a rock into the water.
He **threw** a rock into the water.
She **threw** a rock into the water.
It **threw** a rock into the water.

Andrea **threw** a rock into the water.
Urison **threw** a rock into the water.
Andrea and Urison **threw** a rock into the water.
My cat **threw** a rock into the water.

I **conveyed** a message five minutes ago.
You **conveyed** a message five minutes ago.
We **conveyed** a message five minutes ago.
They **conveyed** a message five minutes ago.
He **conveyed** a message five minutes ago.
She **conveyed** a message five minutes ago.
It **conveyed** a message five minutes ago.
Andrea **conveyed** a message five minutes ago.
Urison **conveyed** a message five minutes ago.
Andrea and Urison **conveyed** a message five minutes ago.
My cat **conveyed** a message five minutes ago.

I **took** my flying lesson this week.
You **took** your flying lesson this week.
We **took** our flying lesson this week.
They **took** their flying lesson this week.
He **took** his flying lesson this week.
She **took** her flying lesson this week.
It **took** its flying lesson this week.
Andrea **took** her flying lesson this week.
Urison **took** his flying lesson this week.
Andrea and Urison **took** their flying lesson this week.
My cat **took** its flying lesson this week.

I **wrote** a letter.
You **wrote** a letter.
We **wrote** a letter.
They **wrote** a letter.
He **wrote** a letter.
She **wrote** a letter.
It **wrote** a letter.
Andrea **wrote** a letter.
Urison **wrote** a letter.
Andrea and Urison **wrote** a letter.

My cat **wrote** a letter.

I **planted** sunflower seeds last month.
You **planted** sunflower seeds last month.
We **planted** sunflower seeds last month.
They **planted** sunflower seeds last month.
He **planted** sunflower seeds last month.
She **planted** sunflower seeds last month.
It **planted** sunflower seeds last month.
Andrea **planted** sunflower seeds last month.
Urison **planted** sunflower seeds last month.
Andrea and Urison **planted** sunflower seeds last month.
My cat **planted** sunflower seeds last month.

Continuiamo:

I **surveyed** human interactions three months ago.
You **surveyed** human interactions three months ago.
We **surveyed** human interactions three months ago.
They **surveyed** human interactions three months ago.
He **surveyed** human interactions three months ago.
She **surveyed** human interactions three months ago.
It **surveyed** human interactions three months ago.
Andrea **surveyed** human interactions three months ago.
Urison **surveyed** human interactions three months ago.
Andrea and Urison **surveyed** human interactions three months ago.
My cat **surveyed** human interactions three months ago.

I **partied** last night.
You **partied** last night.
We **partied** last night.
They **partied** last night.
He **partied** last night.
She **partied** last night.
It **partied** last night.
Andrea **partied** last night.
Urison **partied** last night.
Andrea and Urison **partied** last night.
My cat **partied** last night.

I **watched** the sky last night.
You **watched** the sky last night.
We **watched** the sky last night.
They **watched** the sky last night.
He **watched** the sky last night.
She **watched** the sky last night.
It **watched** the sky last night.
Andrea **watched** the sky last night.
Urison **watched** the sky last night.
Andrea and Urison **watched** the sky last night.
My cat **watched** the sky last night.

I **munched** the apple a few minutes ago.
You **munched** the apple a few minutes ago.
We **munched** the apple a few minutes ago.
They **munched** the apple a few minutes ago.
He **munched** the apple a few minutes ago.
She **munched** the apple a few minutes ago.
It **munched** the apple a few minutes ago.
Andrea **munched** the apple a few minutes ago.
Urison **munched** the apple a few minutes ago.
Andrea and Urison **munched** the apple a few minutes ago.
My cat **munched** the apple a few minutes ago.

I **taught** English yesterday.
You **taught** English yesterday.
We **taught** English yesterday.
They **taught** English yesterday.
He **taught** English yesterday.
She **taught** English yesterday.
It **taught** English yesterday.
Andrea **taught** English yesterday.
Urison **taught** English yesterday.
Andrea and Urison **taught** English yesterday.
My cat **taught** English yesterday.

I **washed** the marsh an hour ago.
You **washed** the marsh an hour ago.

We **washed** the marsh an hour ago.
They **washed** the marsh an hour ago.
He **washed** the marsh an hour ago.
She **washed** the marsh an hour ago.
It **washed** the marsh an hour ago.
Andrea **washed** the marsh an hour ago.
Urison **washed** the marsh an hour ago.
Andrea and Urison **washed** the marsh an hour ago.
My cat **washed** the marsh an hour ago.

I **pushed** the bush two hours ago.
You **pushed** the bush two hours ago.
We **pushed** the bush two hours ago.
They **pushed** the bush two hours ago.
He **pushed** the bush two hours ago.
She **pushed** the bush two hours ago.
It **pushed** the bush two hours ago.
Andrea **pushed** the bush two hours ago.
Urison **pushed** the bush two hours ago.
Andrea and Urison **pushed** the bush two hours ago.
My cat **pushed** the bush two hours ago.

I **dressed** up yesterday.
You **dressed** up yesterday.
We **dressed** up yesterday.
They **dressed** up yesterday.
He **dressed** up yesterday.
She **dressed** up yesterday.
It **dressed** up yesterday.
Andrea **dressed** up yesterday.
Urison **dressed** up yesterday.
Andrea and Urison **dressed** up yesterday.
My cat **dressed** up yesterday.

I **crossed** the crossroad at 11.
You **crossed** the crossroad at 11.
We **crossed** the crossroad at 11.
They **crossed** the crossroad at 11.
He **crossed** the crossroad at 11.

She **crossed** the crossroad at 11.
It **crossed** the crossroad at 11.
Andrea **crossed** the crossroad at 11.
Urison **crossed** the crossroad at 11.
Andrea and Urison **crossed** the crossroad at 11.
My cat **crossed** the crossroad at 11.

I **buzzed** along the runway this morning.
You **buzzed** along the runway this morning.
We **buzzed** along the runway this morning.
They **buzzed** along the runway this morning.
He **buzzed** along the runway this morning.
She **buzzed** along the runway this morning.
It **buzzed** along the runway this morning.
Andrea **buzzed** along the runway this morning.
Urison **buzzed** along the runway this morning.
Andrea and Urison **buzzed** along the runway this morning.
My cat **buzzed** along the runway this morning.

I **jazzed** tonight.
You **jazzed** tonight.
We **jazzed** tonight.
They **jazzed** tonight.
He **jazzed** tonight.
She **jazzed** tonight.
It **jazzed** tonight.
Andrea **jazzed** tonight.
Urison **jazzed** tonight.
Andrea and Urison **jazzed** tonight.
My cat **jazzed** tonight.

I **boxed** my boxes at nine.
You **boxed** my boxes at nine.
We **boxed** my boxes at nine.
They **boxed** my boxes at nine.
He **boxed** my boxes at nine.
She **boxed** my boxes at nine.
It **boxed** my boxes at nine.
Andrea **boxed** my boxes at nine.

Urison **boxed** my boxes at nine.
Andrea and Urison **boxed** my boxes at nine.
My cat **boxed** my boxes at nine.

I **did** my work this morning.
You **did** your work this morning.
We **did** our work this morning.
They **did** their work this morning.
He **did** his work this morning.
She **did** her work this morning.
It **did** its work this morning.
Andrea **did** her work this morning.
Urison **did** his work this morning.
Andrea and Urison **did** their work this morning.
My cat **did** its work this morning.

I **went** all the way to the end.
You **went** all the way to the end.
We **went** all the way to the end.
They **went** all the way to the end.
He **went** all the way to the end.
She **went** all the way to the end.
It **went** all the way to the end.
Andrea **went** all the way to the end.
Urison **went** all the way to the end.
Andrea and Urison **went** all the way to the end.
My cat **went** all the way to the end.

I **had** fun.
You **had** fun.
We **had** fun.
They **had** fun.
He **had** fun.
She **had** fun.
It **had** fun.
Andrea **had** fun.
Urison **had** fun.
Andrea and Urison **had** fun.
My cat **had** fun.

I had vegetables for dinner last night.
You had vegetables for dinner last night.
We had vegetables for dinner last night.
They had vegetables for dinner last night.
He had vegetables for dinner last night.
She had vegetables for dinner last night.
It had vegetables for dinner last night.
Andrea had vegetables for dinner last night.
Urison had vegetables for dinner last night.
Andrea and Urison had vegetables for dinner last night.
My cat had vegetables for dinner last night.

I ran for an hour.
You ran for an hour.
We ran for an hour.
They ran for an hour.
He ran for an hour.
She ran for an hour.
It ran for an hour.
Andrea ran for an hour.
Urison ran for an hour.
Andrea and Urison ran for an hour.
My cat ran for an hour.

I swam before the water was tested.
You swam before the water was tested.
We swam before the water was tested.
They swam before the water was tested.
He swam before the water was tested.
She swam before the water was tested.
It swam before the water was tested.
Andrea swam before the water was tested.
Urison swam before the water was tested.
Andrea and Urison swam before the water was tested.
My cat swam before the water was tested.

3.2 Past Continuous

Per comprendere il past continuous, osserviamo questa frase:

At this time yesterday we **were landing** on the moon.

Il verbo ausiliare è *were* e il verbo principale è *land* (+*ing*). Se cambiamo il soggetto in *she,* allora dobbiamo modificare l'ausiliare in *was*:

At this time yesterday she **was landing** on the moon.

Quando il soggetto è la terza persona o la prima persona singolare, dobbiamo usare *was* come ausiliare. Per tutti gli altri soggetti, usiamo *were*.

Usiamo il past continuous per parlare di:

1. Azioni che stavano accadendo in passato mentre succedeva qualcos'altro:
   - Yesterday, while my cat **was landing** on the moon, NASA called.
   - Last week, while you **were** practicing English, my cat meowed.
   - This morning, the birds **were singing** while the sun **was** rising.
   - While the kids **were playing** in the snow, I **watched**.

2. Azioni che sono state completate in un momento specifico del passato:
   - Yesterday at 10, my cat **was landing** on the moon.
   - An hour ago, you **were** practicing English.
   - This morning at six, the birds **were singing**.
   - Twenty minutes ago, the kids **were playing** snow.

Iniziamo con il past continuous:

I was listening to audiobooks when you called.
You were listening to audiobooks when I called.
We were listening to audiobooks when you called.
They were listening to audiobooks when you called..
He was listening to audiobooks when you called.
She was listening to audiobooks when you called.
It was listening to audiobooks when you called.
Andrea was listening to audiobooks when you called.
Urison was listening to audiobooks when you called.
Andrea and Urison were listening to audiobooks when you called.
My cat was listening to audiobooks when you called.

I was playing when a UFO landed.
You were playing when a UFO landed.
We were playing when a UFO landed.
They were playing when a UFO landed.
He was playing when a UFO landed.
She was playing when a UFO landed.
It was playing when a UFO landed.
Andrea was playing when a UFO landed.
Urison was playing when a UFO landed.
Andrea and Urison were playing when a UFO landed.
My cat was playing when a UFO landed.

I was enjoying life while World War II started.
You were enjoying life while World War II started.
We were enjoying life while World War II started.
They were enjoying life while World War II started.
He was enjoying life while World War II started.
She was enjoying life while World War II started.
It was enjoying life while World War II started.
Andrea was enjoying life while World War II started.
Urison was enjoying life while World War II started.
Andrea and Urison were enjoying life while World War II started.
My cat was enjoying life while World War II started.

I was surveying human behavior when a happy man showed up.
You were surveying human behavior when a happy man showed up.

We **were surveying** human behavior when a happy man showed up.
They **were surveying** human behavior when a happy man showed up.
He **was surveying** human behavior when a happy man showed up.
She **was surveying** human behavior when a happy man showed up.
It **was surveying** human behavior when a happy man showed up.
Andrea **was surveying** human behavior when a happy man showed up.
Urison **was surveying** human behavior when a happy man showed up.
Andrea and Urison **were surveying** human behavior when a happy man showed up.
My cat **was surveying** human behavior when a happy man showed up.

Continuiamo:

I **was studying** at 10 o'clock.
You **were studying** at 10 o'clock.
We **were studying** at 10 o'clock.
They **were studying** at 10 o'clock.
He **was studying** at 10 o'clock.
She **was studying** at 10 o'clock.
It **was studying** at 10 o'clock.
Andrea **was studying** at 10 o'clock.
Urison **was studying** at 10 o'clock.
Andrea and Urison **were studying** at 10 o'clock.
My cat **was studying** at 10 o'clock.

I **was partying** while the music started.
You **were partying** while the music started.
We **were partying** while the music started.
They **were partying** while the music started.
He **was partying** while the music started.
She **was partying** while the music started.
It **was partying** while the music started.
Andrea **was partying** while the music started.

Urison **was partying** while the music started.
Andrea and Urison **were partying** while the music started.
My cat **was partying** while the music started.

I **was teaching** English while he watched.
You **were teaching** English while he watched.
We **were teaching** English while he watched.
They **were teaching** English while he watched.
He **was teaching** English while he watched.
She **was teaching** English while he watched.
It **was teaching** English while he watched.
Andrea **was teaching** English while he watched.
Urison **was teaching** English while he watched.
Andrea and Urison **were teaching** English while he watched.
My cat **was teaching** English while he watched.

I **was watching** stars while a meteor flashed across the sky.
You **were watching** stars while a meteor flashed across the sky.
We **were watching** stars while a meteor flashed across the sky.
They **were watching** stars while a meteor flashed across the sky.
He **was watching** stars while a meteor flashed across the sky.
She **was watching** stars while a meteor flashed across the sky.
It **was watching** stars while a meteor flashed across the sky.
Andrea **was watching** stars while a meteor flashed across the sky.
Urison **was watching** stars while a meteor flashed across the sky.
Andrea and Urison **were watching** stars while a meteor flashed across the sky.
My cat **was watching** stars while a meteor flashed across the sky.

I **was munching** apples while a leaf fell from the tree.
You **were munching** apples while a leaf fell from the tree.
We **were munching** apples while a leaf fell from the tree.
They **were munching** apples while a leaf fell from the tree.
He **was munching** apples while a leaf fell from the tree.
She **was munching** apples while a leaf fell from the tree.
It **was munching** apples while a leaf fell from the tree.
Andrea **was munching** apples while a leaf fell from the tree.
Urison **was munching** apples while a leaf fell from the tree.
Andrea and Urison **were munching** apples while a leaf fell from

69

the tree.
My cat **was munching** apples while a leaf fell from the tree.

I **was washing** the marsh while a fish came.
You **were washing** the marsh while a fish came.
We **were washing** the marsh while a fish came.
They **were washing** the marsh while a fish came.
He **was washing** the marsh while a fish came.
She **was washing** the marsh while a fish came.
It **was washing** the marsh while a fish came.
Andrea **was washing** the marsh while a fish came.
Urison **was washing** the marsh while a fish came.
Andrea and Urison **were washing** the marsh while a fish came.
My cat **was washing** the marsh while a fish came.

I **was pushing** the bush when a guest arrived.
You **were pushing** the bush when a guest arrived.
We **were pushing** the bush when a guest arrived.
They **were pushing** the bush when a guest arrived.
He **was pushing** the bush when a guest arrived.
She **was pushing** the bush when a guest arrived.
It **was pushing** the bush when a guest arrived.
Andrea **was pushing** the bush when a guest arrived.
Urison **was pushing** the bush when a guest arrived.
Andrea and Urison **were pushing** the bush when a guest arrived.
My cat **was pushing** the bush when a guest arrived.

I **was crossing** crossroads when my clock hit 11.
You **were crossing** crossroads when my clock hit 11.
We **were crossing** crossroads when my clock hit 11.
They **were crossing** crossroads when my clock hit 11.
He **was crossing** crossroads when my clock hit 11.
She **was crossing** crossroads when my clock hit 11.
It **was crossing** crossroads when my clock hit 11.
Andrea **was crossing** crossroads when my clock hit 11.
Urison **was crossing** crossroads when my clock hit 11.
Andrea and Urison **were crossing** crossroads when my clock hit 11.
My cat **was crossing** crossroads when my clock hit 11.

I **was buzzing** along the runway while they were playing the game.
You **were buzzing** along the runway while they were playing the game.
We **were buzzing** along the runway while they were playing the game.
They **were buzzing** along the runway while they were playing the game.
He **was buzzing** along the runway while they were playing the game.
She **was buzzing** along the runway while they were playing the game.
It **was buzzing** along the runway while they were playing the game.
Andrea **was buzzing** along the runway while they were playing the game.
Urison **was buzzing** along the runway while they were playing the game.
Andrea and Urison **were buzzing** along the runway while they were playing the game.
My cat **was buzzing** along the runway while they were playing the game.

I **was jazzing** at that time.
You **were jazzing** at that time.
We **were jazzing** at that time.
They **were jazzing** at that time.
He **was jazzing** at that time.
She **was jazzing** at that time.
It **was jazzing** at that time.
Andrea **was jazzing** at that time.
Urison **was jazzing** at that time.
Andrea and Urison **were jazzing** at that time.
My cat **was jazzing** at that time.

While I **was boxing** my boxes, it began.
While you **were boxing** my boxes, it began.
While we **were boxing** my boxes, it began.
While they **were boxing** my boxes, it began.

While he **was boxing** my boxes, it began.
While she **was boxing** my boxes, it began.
While it **was boxing** my boxes, it began.
While Andrea **was boxing** my boxes, it began.
While Urison **was boxing** my boxes, it began.
While Andrea and Urison **were boxing** my boxes, it began.
While my cat **was boxing** my boxes, it began.

I **was doing** my work before three.
You **were doing** your work before three.
We **were doing** our work before three.
They **were doing** their work before three.
He **was doing** his work before three.
She **was doing** her work before three.
It **was doing** its work before three.
Andrea **was doing** her work before three.
Urison **was doing** his work before three.
Andrea and Urison **were doing** their work before three.
My cat **was doing** its work before three.

While I **was going** to work, it started.
While you **were going** to work, it started.
While we **were going** to work, it started.
While they **were going** to work, it started.
While he **was going** to work, it started.
While she **was going** to work, it started.
While it **was going** to work, it started.
While Andrea **was going** to work, it started.
While Urison **was going** to work, it started.
While Andrea and Urison **were going** to work, it started.
While my cat **was going** to work, it started.

While I **was having** fun, more people came.
While you **were having** fun, more people came.
While we **were having** fun, more people came.
While they **were having** fun, more people came.
While he **was having** fun, more people came.
While she **was having** fun, more people came.
While it **was having** fun, more people came.

While Andrea was having fun, more people came.
While Urison was having fun, more people came.
While Andrea and Urison were having fun, more people came.
While my cat was having fun, more people came.

While I was having vegetables, a monk said good.
While you were having vegetables, a monk said good.
While we were having vegetables, a monk said good.
While they were having vegetables, a monk said good.
While he was having vegetables, a monk said good.
While she was having vegetables, a monk said good.
While it was having vegetables, a monk said good.
While Andrea was having vegetables, a monk said good.
While Urison was having vegetables, a monk said good.
While Andrea and Urison were having vegetables, a monk said good.
While my cat was having vegetables, a monk said good.

I was breathing at that time.
You were breathing at that time.
We were breathing at that time.
They were breathing at that time.
He was breathing at that time.
She was breathing at that time.
It was breathing at that time.
Andrea was breathing at that time.
Urison was breathing at that time.
Andrea and Urison were breathing at that time.
My cat was breathing at that time.

I was running while it thundered.
You were running while it thundered.
We were running while it thundered.
They were running while it thundered.
He was running while it thundered.
She was running while it thundered.
It was running while it thundered.
Andrea was running while it thundered.
Urison was running while it thundered.

Andrea and Urison **were running** while it thundered.
My cat **was running** while it thundered.

I **was swimming** while it rained.
You **were swimming** while it rained.
We **were swimming** while it rained.
They **were swimming** while it rained.
He **was swimming** while it rained.
She **was swimming** while it rained.
It **was swimming** while it rained.
Andrea **was swimming** while it rained.
Urison **was swimming** while it rained.
Andrea and Urison **were swimming** while it rained.
My cat **was swimming** while it rained.

I **was cutting** just as it started to rain.
You **were cutting** just as it started to rain.
We **were cutting** just as it started to rain.
They **were cutting** just as it started to rain.
He **was cutting** just as it started to rain.
She **was cutting** just as it started to rain.
It **was cutting** just as it started to rain.
Andrea **was cutting** just as it started to rain.
Urison **was cutting** just as it started to rain.
Andrea and Urison **were cutting** just as it started to rain.
My cat **was cutting** just as it started to rain.

3.3 Past Perfect Continuous

Usiamo il past perfect continuous per azioni che hanno iniziato ad accadere nel passato e sono continuate mentre qualcos'altro è successo nel passato. Ecco un esempio:

Andrea **had been studying** for three hours before she fell asleep.

Il soggetto è *Andrea* e il verbo principale è *study* (*+ing*). La frase ausiliare, *had been*, specifica che l'azione è accaduta nel passato.

Dai un'occhiata a questa frase:

They **had been working** on the moon for three hours when an alien showed up.

Quando il soggetto viene cambiato in *they*, il verbo ausiliare rimane *had been*.

Usiamo il past perfect continuous per parlare di cose accadute nel passato e che sono continuate mentre anche qualcos'altro è accaduto nel passato:
- My cat **had been landing** on the moon when NASA called.
- You **had been** practicing English when my cat meowed.
- The birds **had been singing** for 30 minutes when the sun rose.
- The kids **had been playing** in the snow for 15 minutes when it stopped.

Impariamo il past perfect continuous:

I **had been listening** to audiobooks when a fly showed up.
You **had been listening** to audiobooks when a fly showed up.
We **had been listening** to audiobooks when a fly showed up.
They **had been listening** to audiobooks when a fly showed up..
He **had been listening** to audiobooks when a fly showed up.
She **had been listening** to audiobooks when a fly showed up.
It **had been listening** to audiobooks when a fly showed up.

Andrea **had been listening** to audiobooks when a fly showed up.
Urison **had been listening** to audiobooks when a fly showed up.
Andrea and Urison **had been listening** to audiobooks when a fly showed up.
My cat **had been listening** to audiobooks when a fly showed up.

I **had been playing** the piano when my cat meowed.
You **had been playing** the piano when my cat meowed.
We **had been playing** the piano when my cat meowed.
They **had been playing** the piano when my cat meowed.
He **had been playing** the piano when my cat meowed.
She **had been playing** the piano when my cat meowed.
It **had been playing** the piano when my cat meowed.
Andrea **had been playing** the piano when my cat meowed.
Urison **had been playing** the piano when my cat meowed.
Andrea and Urison **had been playing** the piano when my cat meowed.
My cat **had been playing** the piano when it meowed.

I **had been enjoying** life when WWII started.
You **had been enjoying** life when WWII started.
We **had been enjoying** life when WWII started.
They **had been enjoying** life when WWII started.
He **had been enjoying** life when WWII started.
She **had been enjoying** life when WWII started.
It **had been enjoying** life when WWII started.
Andrea **had been enjoying** life when WWII started.
Urison **had been enjoying** life when WWII started.
Andrea and Urison **had been enjoying** life when WWII started.
My cat **had been enjoying** life when WWII started.

I **had been surveying** human interactions when the march began.
You **had been surveying** human interactions when the march began.
We **had been surveying** human interactions when the march began.
They **had been surveying** human interactions when the march began.
He **had been surveying** human interactions when the march

began.

She **had been surveying** human interactions when the march began.

It **had been surveying** human interactions when the march began.

Andrea **had been surveying** human interactions when the march began.

Urison **had been surveying** human interactions when the march began.

Andrea and Urison **had been surveying** human interactions when the march began.

My cat **had been surveying** human interactions when the march began.

I **had been studying** and won the competition.
You **had been studying** and won the competition.
We **had been studying** and won the competition.
They **had been studying** and won the competition.
He **had been studying** and won the competition.
She **had been studying** and won the competition.
It **had been studying** and won the competition.
Andrea **had been studying** and won the competition.
Urison **had been studying** and won the competition.
Andrea and Urison **had been studying** and won the competition.
My cat **had been studying** and won the competition.

I **had been partying** since the party started.
You **had been partying** since the party started.
We **had been partying** since the party started.
They **had been partying** since the party started.
He **had been partying** since the party started.
She **had been partying** since the party started.
It **had been partying** since the party started.
Andrea **had been partying** since the party started.
Urison **had been partying** since the party started.
Andrea and Urison **had been partying** since the party started.
My cat **had been partying** since the party started.

È il past perfect continuous che stiamo imparando in questo momento.

I **had been teaching** English since the opening of this school.
You **had been teaching** English since the opening of this school.
We **had been teaching** English since the opening of this school.
They **had been teaching** English since the opening of this school.
He **had been teaching** English since the opening of this school.
She **had been teaching** English since the opening of this school.
It **had been teaching** English since the opening of this school.
Andrea **had been teaching** English since the opening of this school.
Urison **had been teaching** English since the opening of this school.
Andrea and Urison **had been teaching** English since the opening of this school.
My cat **had been teaching** English since the opening of this school.

I **had been watching** the sky all night.
You **had been watching** the sky all night.
We **had been watching** the sky all night.
They **had been watching** the sky all night.
He **had been watching** the sky all night.
She **had been watching** the sky all night.
It **had been watching** the sky all night.
Andrea **had been watching** the sky all night.
Urison **had been watching** the sky all night.
Andrea and Urison **had been watching** the sky all night.
My cat **had been watching** the sky all night.

I **had been munching** apples when a fly showed up.
You **had been munching** apples when a fly showed up.
We **had been munching** apples when a fly showed up.
They **had been munching** apples when a fly showed up.
He **had been munching** apples when a fly showed up.
She **had been munching** apples when a fly showed up.
It **had been munching** apples when a fly showed up.
Andrea **had been munching** apples when a fly showed up.
Urison **had been munching** apples when a fly showed up.
Andrea and Urison **had been munching** apples when a fly showed

up.

My cat had been munching apples when a fly showed up.

I had been washing the marsh before a fish came.
You had been washing the marsh before a fish came.
We had been washing the marsh before a fish came.
They had been washing the marsh before a fish came.
He had been washing the marsh before a fish came.
She had been washing the marsh before a fish came.
It had been washing the marsh before a fish came.
Andrea had been washing the marsh before a fish came.
Urison had been washing the marsh before a fish came.
Andrea and Urison had been washing the marsh before a fish
came.
My cat had been washing the marsh before a fish came.

Esegui più esercizi per fissare il past perfect continuous nel tuo
subconscio:

I had been pushing the bush before class started.
You had been pushing the bush before class started.
We had been pushing the bush before class started.
They had been pushing the bush before class started.
He had been pushing the bush before class started.
She had been pushing the bush before class started.
It had been pushing the bush before class started.
Andrea had been pushing the bush before class started.
Urison had been pushing the bush before class started.
Andrea and Urison had been pushing the bush before class
started.
My cat had been pushing the bush before class started.

I had been dressing before it showed up.
You had been dressing before it showed up.
We had been dressing before it showed up.
They had been dressing before it showed up.
He had been dressing before it showed up.
She had been dressing before it showed up.
It had been dressing before it showed up.

Andrea **had been dressing** before it showed up.
Urison **had been dressing** before it showed up.
Andrea and Urison **had been dressing** before it showed up.
My cat **had been dressing** before it showed up.

I **had been pressing** the button before the elevator came.
You **had been pressing** the button before the elevator came.
We **had been pressing** the button before the elevator came.
They **had been pressing** the button before the elevator came.
He **had been pressing** the button before the elevator came.
She **had been pressing** the button before the elevator came.
It **had been pressing** the button before the elevator came.
Andrea **had been pressing** the button before the elevator came.
Urison **had been pressing** the button before the elevator came.
Andrea and Urison **had been pressing** the button before the elevator came.
My cat **had been pressing** the button before the elevator came.

I **had been buzzing** along the runway when the plane took off.
You **had been buzzing** along the runway when the plane took off.
We **had been buzzing** along the runway when the plane took off.
They **had been buzzing** along the runway when the plane took off.
He **had been buzzing** along the runway when the plane took off.
She **had been buzzing** along the runway when the plane took off.
It **had been buzzing** along the runway when the plane took off.
Andrea **had been buzzing** along the runway when the plane took off.
Urison **had been buzzing** along the runway when the plane took off.
Andrea and Urison **had been buzzing** along the runway when the plane took off.
My cat **had been buzzing** along the runway when the plane took off.

I **had been jazzing** when the show started.
You **had been jazzing** when the show started.
We **had been jazzing** when the show started.
They **had been jazzing** when the show started.
He **had been jazzing** when the show started.

She **had been jazzing** when the show started.
It **had been jazzing** when the show started.
Andrea **had been jazzing** when the show started.
Urison **had been jazzing** when the show started.
Andrea and Urison **had been jazzing** when the show started.
My cat **had been jazzing** when the show started.

I **had been boxing** my boxes when a beetle buzzed by.
You **had been boxing** my boxes when a beetle buzzed by.
We **had been boxing** my boxes when a beetle buzzed by.
They **had been boxing** my boxes when a beetle buzzed by.
He **had been boxing** my boxes when a beetle buzzed by.
She **had been boxing** my boxes when a beetle buzzed by.
It **had been boxing** my boxes when a beetle buzzed by.
Andrea **had been boxing** my boxes when a beetle buzzed by.
Urison **had been boxing** my boxes when a beetle buzzed by.
Andrea and Urison **had been boxing** my boxes when a beetle buzzed by.
My cat **had been boxing** my boxes when a beetle buzzed by.

I **had been doing** my work when it snowed.
You **had been doing** your work when it snowed.
We **had been doing** our work when it snowed.
They **had been doing** their work when it snowed.
He **had been doing** his work when it snowed.
She **had been doing** her work when it snowed.
It **had been doing** its work when it snowed.
Andrea **had been doing** her work when it snowed.
Urison **had been doing** his work when it snowed.
Andrea and Urison **had been doing** their work when it snowed.
My cat **had been doing** its work when it snowed.

I **had been going** around when the wind started.
You **had been going** around when the wind started.
We **had been going** around when the wind started.
They **had been going** around when the wind started.
He **had been going** around when the wind started.
She **had been going** around when the wind started.
It **had been going** around when the wind started.

Andrea **had been going** around when the wind started.
Urison **had been going** around when the wind started.
Andrea and Urison **had been going** around when the wind started.
My cat **had been going** around when the wind started.

I **had been having** fun when the party started.
You **had been having** fun when the party started.
We **had been having** fun when the party started.
They **had been having** fun when the party started.
He **had been having** fun when the party started.
She **had been having** fun when the party started.
It **had been having** fun when the party started.
Andrea **had been having** fun when the party started.
Urison **had been having** fun when the party started.
Andrea and Urison **had been having** fun when the party started.
My cat **had been having** fun when the party started.

I **had been having** vegetables for dinner for three years.
You **had been having** vegetables for dinner for three years.
We **had been having** vegetables for dinner for three years.
They **had been having** vegetables for dinner for three years.
He **had been having** vegetables for dinner for three years.
She **had been having** vegetables for dinner for three years.
It **had been having** vegetables for dinner for three years.
Andrea **had been having** vegetables for dinner for three years.
Urison **had been having** vegetables for dinner for three years.
Andrea and Urison **had been having** vegetables for dinner for
three years.
My cat **had been having** vegetables for dinner for three years.

I **had been running** when it thundered.
You **had been running** when it thundered.
We **had been running** when it thundered.
They **had been running** when it thundered.
He **had been running** when it thundered.
She **had been running** when it thundered.
It **had been running** when it thundered.
Andrea **had been running** when it thundered.
Urison **had been running** when it thundered.

Andrea and Urison **had been running** when it thundered.
My cat **had been running** when it thundered.

I **had been swimming** when a turtle came.
You **had been swimming** when a turtle came.
We **had been swimming** when a turtle came.
They **had been swimming** when a turtle came.
He **had been swimming** when a turtle came.
She **had been swimming** when a turtle came.
It **had been swimming** when a turtle came.
Andrea **had been swimming** when a turtle came.
Urison **had been swimming** when a turtle came.
Andrea and Urison **had been swimming** when a turtle came.
My cat **had been swimming** when a turtle came.

3.4 Past Perfect

Osserva questa frase:

Andrea **had studied** for three hours before she fell asleep.

Il soggetto è *Andrea* e il verbo principale è *studied* (il participio passato di *study)*. Il verbo ausiliare *had* ci comunica che questi eventi sono accaduti nel passato.

Ora, diamo un'occhiata a questa frase:

They **had studied** for three hours before they fell asleep.

Se il soggetto diventa *they*, il verbo ausiliare rimane *had*.

Usiamo il past perfect per parlare di azioni accadute nel passato prima che succedesse qualcos'altro:
- My cat **had landed** on the moon when NASA called.
- You **had practiced** English when my cat meowed.
- The birds **had sung** for 30 minutes when the sun rose.
- The kids **had played** in the snow for 15 minutes when it stopped.

Impariamo il past perfect:

I **had listened** to audiobooks before a fly showed up.
You **had listened** to audiobooks before a fly showed up.
We **had listened** to audiobooks before a fly showed up.
They **had listened** to audiobooks before a fly showed up.
He **had listened** to audiobooks before a fly showed up.
She **had listened** to audiobooks before a fly showed up.
It **had listened** to audiobooks before a fly showed up.
Andrea **had listened** to audiobooks before a fly showed up.
Urison **had listened** to audiobooks before a fly showed up.
Andrea and Urison **had listened** to audiobooks before a fly showed up.
My cat **had listened** to audiobooks before a fly showed up.

I **had played** the piano before my cat meowed.
You **had played** the piano before my cat meowed.
We **had played** the piano before my cat meowed.
They **had played** the piano before my cat meowed.
He **had played** the piano before my cat meowed.
She **had played** the piano before my cat meowed.
It **had played** the piano before my cat meowed.
Andrea **had played** the piano before my cat meowed.
Urison **had played** the piano before my cat meowed.
Andrea and Urison **had played** the piano before my cat meowed.
My cat **had played** the piano before my cat meowed.

I **had enjoyed** life before WWII started.
You **had enjoyed** life before WWII started.
We **had enjoyed** life before WWII started.
They **had enjoyed** life before WWII started.
He **had enjoyed** life before WWII started.
She **had enjoyed** life before WWII started.
It **had enjoyed** life before WWII started.
Andrea **had enjoyed** life before WWII started.
Urison **had enjoyed** life before WWII started.
Andrea and Urison **had enjoyed** life before WWII started.
My cat **had enjoyed** life before WWII started.

I **had surveyed** human interactions before the march started.
You **had surveyed** human interactions before the march started.
We **had surveyed** human interactions before the march started.
They **had surveyed** human interactions before the march started.
He **had surveyed** human interactions before the march started.
She **had surveyed** human interactions before the march started.
It **had surveyed** human interactions before the march started.
Andrea **had surveyed** human interactions before the march started.
Urison **had surveyed** human interactions before the march started.
Andrea and Urison **had surveyed** human interactions before the march started.
My cat **had surveyed** human interactions before the march started.

I **had studied** before I won the competition.

You **had studied** before I won the competition.
We **had studied** before I won the competition.
They **had studied** before I won the competition.
He **had studied** before I won the competition.
She **had studied** before I won the competition.
It **had studied** before I won the competition.
Andrea **had studied** before I won the competition.
Urison **had studied** before I won the competition.
Andrea and Urison **had studied** before I won the competition.
My cat **had studied** before I won the competition.

Esegui più esercizi per fissare il past perfect nel tuo subconscio:

I **had partied** before the party started.
You **had partied** before the party started.
We **had partied** before the party started.
They **had partied** before the party started.
He **had partied** before the party started.
She **had partied** before the party started.
It **had partied** before the party started.
Andrea **had partied** before the party started.
Urison **had partied** before the party started.
Andrea and Urison **had partied** before the party started.
My cat **had partied** before the party started.

I **had taught** English before the opening of this school.
You **had taught** English before the opening of this school.
We **had taught** English before the opening of this school.
They **had taught** English before the opening of this school.
He **had taught** English before the opening of this school.
She **had taught** English before the opening of this school.
It **had taught** English before the opening of this school.
Andrea **had taught** English before the opening of this school.
Urison **had taught** English before the opening of this school.
Andrea and Urison **had taught** English before the opening of this school.
My cat **had taught** English before the opening of this school.

I **had watched** the sky before a meteor struck.

You **had watched** the sky before a meteor struck.
We **had watched** the sky before a meteor struck.
They **had watched** the sky before a meteor struck.
He **had watched** the sky before a meteor struck.
She **had watched** the sky before a meteor struck.
It **had watched** the sky before a meteor struck.
Andrea **had watched** the sky before a meteor struck.
Urison **had watched** the sky before a meteor struck.
Andrea and Urison **had watched** the sky before a meteor struck.
My cat **had watched** the sky before a meteor struck.

I **had munched** apples before a fly showed up.
You **had munched** apples before a fly showed up.
We **had munched** apples before a fly showed up.
They **had munched** apples before a fly showed up.
He **had munched** apples before a fly showed up.
She **had munched** apples before a fly showed up.
It **had munched** apples before a fly showed up.
Andrea **had munched** apples before a fly showed up.
Urison **had munched** apples before a fly showed up.
Andrea and Urison **had munched** apples before a fly showed up.
My cat **had munched** apples before a fly showed up.

I **had washed** the marsh before a fish came.
You **had washed** the marsh before a fish came.
We **had washed** the marsh before a fish came.
They **had washed** the marsh before a fish came.
He **had washed** the marsh before a fish came.
She **had washed** the marsh before a fish came.
It **had washed** the marsh before a fish came.
Andrea **had washed** the marsh before a fish came.
Urison **had washed** the marsh before a fish came.
Andrea and Urison **had washed** the marsh before a fish came.
My cat **had washed** the marsh before a fish came.

I **had pushed** the bush before class started.
You **had pushed** the bush before class started.
We **had pushed** the bush before class started.
They **had pushed** the bush before class started.

He **had pushed** the bush before class started.
She **had pushed** the bush before class started.
It **had pushed** the bush before class started.
Andrea **had pushed** the bush before class started.
Urison **had pushed** the bush before class started.
Andrea and Urison **had pushed** the bush before class started.
My cat **had pushed** the bush before class started.

I **had dressed** before it showed up.
You **had dressed** before it showed up.
We **had dressed** before it showed up.
They **had dressed** before it showed up.
He **had dressed** before it showed up.
She **had dressed** before it showed up.
It **had dressed** before it showed up.
Andrea **had dressed** before it showed up.
Urison **had dressed** before it showed up.
Andrea and Urison **had dressed** before it showed up.
My cat **had dressed** before it showed up.

I **had pressed** the button before the elevator came.
You **had pressed** the button before the elevator came.
We **had pressed** the button before the elevator came.
They **had pressed** the button before the elevator came.
He **had pressed** the button before the elevator came.
She **had pressed** the button before the elevator came.
It **had pressed** the button before the elevator came.
Andrea **had pressed** the button before the elevator came.
Urison **had pressed** the button before the elevator came.
Andrea and Urison **had pressed** the button before the elevator came.
My cat **had pressed** the button before the elevator came.

I **had buzzed** along the runway before the plane took off.
You **had buzzed** along the runway before the plane took off.
We **had buzzed** along the runway before the plane took off.
They **had buzzed** along the runway before the plane took off.
He **had buzzed** along the runway before the plane took off.
She **had buzzed** along the runway before the plane took off.

It **had buzzed** along the runway before the plane took off.
Andrea **had buzzed** along the runway before the plane **took** off.
Urison **had buzzed** along the runway before the plane took off.
Andrea and Urison **had buzzed** along the runway before the plane took off.
My cat **had buzzed** along the runway before the plane took off.

I **had jazzed** before the show started.
You **had jazzed** before the show started.
We **had jazzed** before the show started.
They **had jazzed** before the show started.
He **had jazzed** before the show started.
She **had jazzed** before the show started.
It **had jazzed** before the show started.
Andrea **had jazzed** before the show started.
Urison **had jazzed** before the show started.
Andrea and Urison **had jazzed** before the show started.
My cat **had jazzed** before the show started.

I **had boxed** my boxes before a puppy came by.
You **had boxed** my boxes before a puppy came by.
We **had boxed** my boxes before a puppy came by.
They **had boxed** my boxes before a puppy came by.
He **had boxed** my boxes before a puppy came by.
She **had boxed** my boxes before a puppy came by.
It **had boxed** my boxes before a puppy came by.
Andrea **had boxed** my boxes before a puppy came by.
Urison **had boxed** my boxes before a puppy came by.
Andrea and Urison **had boxed** my boxes before a puppy came by.
My cat **had boxed** my boxes before a puppy came by.

I **had done** my work before my boss showed up.
You **had done** your work before my boss showed up.
We **had done** our work before my boss showed up.
They **had done** their work before my boss showed up.
He **had done** his work before my boss showed up.
She **had done** her work before my boss showed up.
It **had done** its work before my boss showed up.
Andrea **had done** her work before my boss showed up.

Urison **had done** his work before my boss showed up.
Andrea and Urison **had done** their work before my boss showed up.
My cat **had done** its work before my boss showed up.

I **had gone** around before the wind started.
You **had gone** around before the wind started.
We **had gone** around before the wind started.
They **had gone** around before the wind started.
He **had gone** around before the wind started.
She **had gone** around before the wind started.
It **had gone** around before the wind started.
Andrea **had gone** around before the wind started.
Urison **had gone** around before the wind started.
Andrea and Urison **had gone** around before the wind started.
My cat **had gone** around before the wind started.

Ora osserva attentamente queste frasi.

I **had had** fun before the party started.
You **had had** fun before the party started.
We **had had** fun before the party started.
They **had had** fun before the party started.
He **had had** fun before the party started.
She **had had** fun before the party started.
It **had had** fun before the party started.
Andrea **had had** fun before the party started.
Urison **had had** fun before the party started.
Andrea and Urison **had had** fun before the party started.
My cat **had had** fun before the party started.

I **had had** vegetables before dinner.
You **had had** vegetables before dinner.
We **had had** vegetables before dinner.
They **had had** vegetables before dinner.
He **had had** vegetables before dinner.
She **had had** vegetables before dinner.
It **had had** vegetables before dinner.
Andrea **had had** vegetables before dinner.

Urison **had had** vegetables before dinner.
Andrea and Urison **had had** vegetables before dinner.
My cat **had had** vegetables before dinner.

I **had run** before it thundered.
You **had run** before it thundered.
We **had run** before it thundered.
They **had run** before it thundered.
He **had run** before it thundered.
She **had run** before it thundered.
It **had run** before it thundered.
Andrea **had run** before it thundered.
Urison **had run** before it thundered.
Andrea and Urison **had run** before it thundered.
My cat **had run** before it thundered.

I **had swum** before a turtle came
You **had swum** before a turtle came
We **had swum** before a turtle came
They **had swum** before a turtle came
He **had swum** before a turtle came
She **had swum** before a turtle came
It **had swum** before a turtle came
Andrea **had swum** before a turtle came
Urison **had swum** before a turtle came
Andrea and Urison **had swum** before a turtle came
My cat **had swum** before a turtle came

I said that I **had** never **flown** to the moon before.
You said that you **had** never **flown** to the moon before.
We said that we **had** never **flown** to the moon before.
They said that they **had** never **flown** to the moon before.
He said that he **had** never **flown** to the moon before.
She said that she **had** never **flown** to the moon before.
It said that it **had** never **flown** to the moon before.
Andrea said that she **had** never **flown** to the moon before.
Urison said that he **had** never **flown** to the moon before.
Andrea and Urison said that they **had** never **flown** to the moon before.

My cat said that it **had** never **flown** to the moon before.

I wondered why it **had been** so cold.
You wondered why it **had been** so cold.
We wondered why it **had been** so cold.
They wondered why it **had been** so cold.
He wondered why it **had been** so cold.
She wondered why it **had been** so cold.
It wondered why it **had been** so cold.
Andrea wondered why it **had been** so cold.
Urison wondered why it **had been** so cold.
Andrea and Urison wondered why it **had been** so cold.
My cat wondered why it **had been** so cold.

If I **had landed** on Venus, I would have been fried.
If you **had landed** on Venus, you would have been fried.
If we **had landed** on Venus, we would have been fried.
If they **had landed** on Venus, they would have been fried.
If he **had landed** on Venus, he would have been fried.
If she **had landed** on Venus, she would have been fried.
If it **had landed** on Venus, it would have been fried.
If Andrea **had landed** on Venus, she would have been fried.
If Urison **had landed** on Venus, he would have been fried.
If Andrea and Urison **had landed** on Venus, they would have been fried.
If my cat **had landed** on Venus, it would have been fried.

Capitolo 4: Futuro

4.1 Simple Future

Per imparare il tempo futuro, osserva questa frase:

I **will study** for the test.

Si tratta di qualcosa che ho promesso di fare in futuro.

Usiamo il simple future:

1. Per fare delle promesse:
   * I **will study** for the test.
   * Promise you **will bring** it back.
   * I **will walk** to school with you.
   * I **will be** there at five.

2. Per prevedere qualcosa che accadrà in futuro:
   * Looks like it **is going** to **be** sunny tomorrow.
   * It **will be** sunny tomorrow.
   * She **is going** to **be** a good driver.
   * Andrea **is going** to pass the test.
   * Urison **is going** to **be** an astronomer.

3. Per proporre un'offerta:
   * **Shall** we **dance**?
   * **Shall** we **sing**?
   * **Shall** we **go** by car?
   * **Shall** I **finish** it for you?

4. Per parlare di accordi fissi:
   * When **are** you **starting**?
   * I **am starting** next week.

- When **is** the CEO **visiting** the store?
- The CEO **is visiting** on Tuesday.

Ora, diamo un'occhiata a questa frase:

We **will land** on the moon.

Se modifichiamo il soggetto in *she*, tutto il resto rimane uguale:

She **will land** on the moon.

Questo esempio promette che succederà qualcosa in futuro. Per qualcosa che accadrà nel futuro, usiamo *will* + *verbo*.

Ora impariamo il simple future:

I **will land** on the moon.
We **will land** on the moon.
You **will land** on the moon.
They **will land** on the moon.
He **will land** on the moon.
She **will land** on the moon.
It **will land** on the moon.
Andrea **will land** on the moon.
Urison **will land** on the moon.
Andrea and Urison **will land** on the moon.
My cat **will land** on the moon.

I **will listen** to audiobooks every day.
You **will listen** to audiobooks every day.
We **will listen** to audiobooks every day.
They **will listen** to audiobooks every day.
He **will listen** to audiobooks every day.
She **will listen** to audiobooks every day.
It **will listen** to audiobooks every day.
Andrea **will listen** to audiobooks every day.
Urison **will listen** to audiobooks every day.
Andrea and Urison **will listen** to audiobooks every day.

My cat **will listen** to audiobooks every day.

I **will wake up** at seven tomorrow.
You **will wake up** at seven tomorrow.
We **will wake up** at seven tomorrow.
They **will wake up** at seven tomorrow.
He **will wake up** at seven tomorrow.
She **will wake up** at seven tomorrow.
It **will wake up** at seven tomorrow.
Andrea **will wake up** at seven tomorrow.
Urison **will wake up** at seven tomorrow.
Andrea and Urison **will wake up** at seven tomorrow.
My cat **will wake up** at seven tomorrow.

I **will play** every day.
You **will play** every day.
We **will play** every day.
They **will play** every day.
He **will play** every day.
She **will play** every day.
It **will play** every day.
Andrea **will play** every day.
Urison **will play** every day.
Andrea and Urison **will play** every day.
My cat **will play** every day.

I **will enjoy** life every day.
You **will enjoy** life every day.
We **will enjoy** life every day.
They **will enjoy** life every day.
He **will enjoy** life every day.
She **will enjoy** life every day.
It **will enjoy** life every day.
Andrea **will enjoy** life every day.
Urison **will enjoy** life every day.
Andrea and Urison **will enjoy** life every day.
My cat **will enjoy** life every day.

Esegui più esercizi per acquisire questo tempo all'interno del tuo subconscio:

I **will survey** next week.
You **will survey** next week.
We **will survey** next week.
They **will survey** next week.
He **will survey** next week.
She **will survey** next week.
It **will survey** next week.
Andrea **will survey** next week.
Urison **will survey** next week.
Andrea and Urison **will survey** next week.
My cat **will survey** next week.

I **will study** tonight.
You **will study** tonight.
We **will study** tonight.
They **will study** tonight.
He **will study** tonight.
She **will study** tonight.
It **will study** tonight.
Andrea **will study** tonight.
Urison **will study** tonight.
Andrea and Urison **will study** tonight.
My cat **will study** tonight.

I **will stay** home for a week.
You **will stay** home for a week.
We **will stay** home for a week.
They **will stay** home for a week.
He **will stay** home for a week.
She **will stay** home for a week.
It **will stay** home for a week.
Andrea **will stay** home for a week.
Urison **will stay** home for a week.
Andrea and Urison **will stay** home for a week.
My cat **will stay** home for a week.

I **will buy** lunch for a week.

You will buy lunch for a week.
We will buy lunch for a week.
They will buy lunch for a week.
He will buy lunch for a week.
She will buy lunch for a week.
It will buy lunch for a week.
Andrea will buy lunch for a week.
Urison will buy lunch for a week.
Andrea and Urison will buy lunch for a week.
My cat will buy lunch for a week.

Per qualcosa che potrebbe accadere in futuro, usiamo *be going to* + *verbo*.

I am going to party tonight.
You are going to party tonight.
We are going to party tonight.
They are going to party tonight.
He is going to party tonight.
She is going to party tonight.
It is going to party tonight.
Andrea is going to party tonight.
Urison is going to party tonight.
Andrea and Urison are going to party tonight.
My cat is going to party tonight.

I will fly tomorrow.
You will fly tomorrow.
We will fly tomorrow.
They will fly tomorrow.
He will fly tomorrow.
She will fly tomorrow.
It will fly tomorrow.
Andrea will fly tomorrow.
Urison will fly tomorrow.
Andrea and Urison will fly tomorrow.
My cat will fly tomorrow.

I am going to teach English.

You **are going to teach** English.
We **are going to teach** English.
They **are going to teach** English.
He **is going to teach** English.
She **is going to teach** English.
It **is going to teach** English.
Andrea **is going to teach** English.
Urison **is going to teach** English.
Andrea and Urison **are going to teach** English.
My cat **is going to teach** English.

I **will watch** the sky tonight.
You **will watch** the sky tonight.
We **will watch** the sky tonight.
They **will watch** the sky tonight.
He **will watch** the sky tonight.
She **will watch** the sky tonight.
It **will watch** the sky tonight.
Andrea **will watch** the sky tonight.
Urison **will watch** the sky tonight.
Andrea and Urison **will watch** the sky tonight.
My cat **will watch** the sky tonight.

I **will munch** apples every day.
You **will munch** apples every day.
We **will munch** apples every day.
They **will munch** apples every day.
He **will munch** apples every day.
She **will munch** apples every day.
It **will munch** apples every day.
Andrea **will munch** apples every day.
Urison **will munch** apples every day.
Andrea and Urison **will munch** apples every day.
My cat **will munch** apples every day.

I **will wash** the marsh.
You **will wash** the marsh.
We **will wash** the marsh.
They **will wash** the marsh.

He will wash the marsh.
She will wash the marsh.
It will wash the marsh.
Andrea will wash the marsh.
Urison will wash the marsh.
Andrea and Urison will wash the marsh.
My cat will wash the marsh.

I will push the bush
You will push the bush.
We will push the bush.
They will push the bush.
He will push the bush.
She will push the bush.
It will push the bush.
Andrea will push the bush.
Urison will push the bush.
Andrea and Urison will push the bush.
My cat will push the bush.

I will cross the crossroad.
You will cross the crossroad.
We will cross the crossroad.
They will cross the crossroad.
He will cross the crossroad.
She will cross the crossroad.
It will cross the crossroad.
Andrea will cross the crossroad.
Urison will cross the crossroad.
Andrea and Urison will cross the crossroad.
My cat will cross the crossroad.

Invece di *will,* possiamo usare anche *going to*, per esprimere
un'azione che si svolgerà nel futuro:

I am going to cross the crossroad.
You are going to cross the crossroad.
We are going to cross the crossroad.
They are going to cross the crossroad.

He **is going to cross** the crossroad.
She **is going to cross** the crossroad.
It **is going to cross** the crossroad.
Andrea **is going to cross** the crossroad.
Urison **is going to cross** the crossroad.
Andrea and Urison **are going to cross** the crossroad.
My cat **is going to cross** the crossroad.

I **will buzz** along the runway.
You **will buzz** along the runway.
We **will buzz** along the runway.
They **will buzz** along the runway.
He **will buzz** along the runway.
She **will buzz** along the runway.
It **will buzz** along the runway.
Andrea **will buzz** along the runway.
Urison **will buzz** along the runway.
Andrea and Urison **will buzz** along the runway.
My cat **will buzz** along the runway.

I **will jazz** today.
You **will jazz** today.
We **will jazz** today.
They **will jazz** today.
He **will jazz** today.
She **will jazz** today.
It **will jazz** today.
Andrea **will jazz** today.
Urison **will jazz** today.
Andrea and Urison **will jazz** today.
My cat **will jazz** today.

I **will box** my boxes for vacation.
You **will box** my boxes for vacation.
We **will box** my boxes for vacation.
They **will box** my boxes for vacation.
He **will box** my boxes for vacation.
She **will box** my boxes for vacation.
It **will box** my boxes for vacation.

Andrea will box my boxes for vacation.
Urison will box my boxes for vacation.
Andrea and Urison will box my boxes for vacation.
My cat will box my boxes for vacation.

I will relax on my relaxation bench today.
You will relax on my relaxation bench today.
We will relax on my relaxation bench today.
They will relax on my relaxation bench today.
He will relax on my relaxation bench today.
She will relax on my relaxation bench today.
It will relax on my relaxation bench today.
Andrea will relax on my relaxation bench today.
Urison will relax on my relaxation bench today.
Andrea and Urison will relax on my relaxation bench today.
My cat will relax on my relaxation bench today.

I will fix my friend's car once a while.
You will fix my friend's car once a while.
We will fix my friend's car once a while.
They will fix my friend's car once a while.
He will fix my friend's car once a while.
She will fix my friend's car once a while.
It will fix my friend's car once a while.
Andrea will fix my friend's car once a while.
Urison will fix my friend's car once a while.
Andrea and Urison will fix my friend's car once a while.
My cat will fix my friend's car once a while.

I will do my work.
You will do your work.
We will do our work.
They will do their work.
He will do his work.
She will do her work.
It will do its work.
Andrea will do her work.
Urison will do his work.
Andrea and Urison will do their work.

My cat **will do** its work.

I **will go to** work by foot.
You **will go to** work by foot.
We **will go to** work by foot.
They **will go to** work by foot.
He **will go to** work by foot.
She **will go to** work by foot.
It **will go to** work by foot.
Andrea **will go to** work by foot.
Urison **will go to** work by foot.
Andrea and Urison **will go to** work by foot.
My cat **will go to** work by foot.

I **will have** fun today.
You **will have** fun today.
We **will have** fun today.
They **will have** fun today.
He **will have** fun today.
She **will have** fun today.
It **will have** fun today.
Andrea **will have** fun today.
Urison **will have** fun today.
Andrea and Urison **will have** fun today.
My cat **will have** fun today.

I **will have** water.
You **will have** water.
We **will have** water.
They **will have** water.
He **will have** water.
She **will have** water.
It **will have** water.
Andrea **will have** water.
Urison **will have** water.
Andrea and Urison **will have** water.
My cat **will have** water.

I **will have** vegetables for dinner.

You **will have** vegetables for dinner.
We **will have** vegetables for dinner.
They **will have** vegetables for dinner.
He **will have** vegetables for dinner.
She **will have** vegetables for dinner.
It **will have** vegetables for dinner.
Andrea **will have** vegetables for dinner.
Urison **will have** vegetables for dinner.
Andrea and Urison **will have** vegetables for dinner.
My cat **will have** vegetables for dinner.

I **will be** here.
You **will be** awesome.
We **will be** happy.
They **will be** perfect.
He **will be** a student.
My cat **will be** a helper.
Computers **will be** made with alien technologies.

Congratulazioni! Termineremo l'apprendimento del simple future tra un attimo. Festeggia praticando altri esercizi.

I **will be** happy.
You **will be** tall.
We **will be** shiny.
They **will be** on Earth.
He **will be** a pilot.
She **will be** a nurse.
It **will be** cold.

Usiamo *shall* nelle situazioni formali per fare delle offerte:

Shall we **dance**?
Shall we **sing**?
Shall we **go** by car?
Shall I **finish** it for you?
Shall we **go** to a movie tonight?
Shall we **land** on the moon?
Shall I **bring** food to the party?

We **Shall** see.

Il simple present e il present continuous possono anche essere utilizzati per esprimere il tempo futuro. Li usiamo per accordi fissi che sono programmati per accadere in un momento futuro. I lettori possono scoprire se sono tempi presenti o futuri, osservando il contesto.

The plane **lands** at five.
I **fly** on Monday.
When **are** you **starting**?
When **is** the CEO **visiting** the store?
We **are flying** tomorrow.
You **are leaving** in two hours.
They **are holding** a meeting tonight.

Usiamo *about to* + *verbo* per indicare qualcosa che non è stato ancora avviato, ma inizierà in qualsiasi momento del futuro:

I **am about to get** started.
We **are about to land**.
They **are about to finish**.
He **is about to begin**.
She **is about to study**.

Usiamo la forma *to be* + *to* + verbo per riferire qualcosa che accadrà in futuro in base ad una regola o un'istruzione.

I **am to get** it **done** in three days.
We **are to land** in Atlanta.
They **are to finish** in 10 minutes.
He **is to fly** for 12 hours.
She **is to study** until noon.
You **are to go** straight to the forest.

4.2 Future Continuous

Per imparare il Future continuous, osserva la seguente frase:

Tomorrow at this time, I **will be studying** for the test.

Il Future continuous indica un'azione in corso che avverrà nel futuro. Nell'esempio precedente, studiare è qualcosa che farò domani a quest'ora.

Usiamo il future continuous:

1. Per indicare che saremo nel mezzo di un'azione in un certo momento del futuro:
   - Next Monday at 10, I **will be taking** the test.
   - Tomorrow at 7:50, we **will be walking** to school.
   - I **will be teaching** grammar at the conference next week.
   - They **will be singing** at the show tonight.

2. Per parlare di cose che stanno succedendo in questo momento e che dovrebbero continuare nel futuro:
   - An hour from now I **will** still **be taking** the test.
   - Tomorrow by eight we **will** still **be walking**.
   - Next week I **will** still **be teaching** grammar.
   - Tonight at 10 they **will** still **be singing** at the show.

3. Per indovinare cosa succederà in futuro:
   - She **will be getting** her driver's license soon.
   - Andrea **will be getting** an A on the test.
   - They **will be buying** a house soon.
   - The CEO **will be visiting** soon.

4. Per chiedere gentilmente i piani futuri di qualcuno:
   - **Will** you **be picking** milk up on the way home?
   - **Are** you **going** to **be picking** milk up on the way home?
   - **Will** you **be** driving or **walking**?

- **Are** you **going** to **be** driving or **walking**?

Dai un'occhiata a questa frase:

When you wake up tomorrow, we **will be landing** on the moon.

Ora, se cambiamo il soggetto in *she*, tutto il resto rimane identico:

When you wake up tomorrow, she **will be landing** on the moon.

Questo esempio indica che qualcuno sarà nel mezzo di un'azione in futuro.

Ora impariamo il future continuous.

When you wake up tomorrow, I **will be landing** on the moon.
When you wake up tomorrow, we **will be landing** on the moon.
When you wake up tomorrow, you **will be landing** on the moon.
When you wake up tomorrow, they **will be landing** on the moon.
When you wake up tomorrow, she **will be landing** on the moon.
When you wake up tomorrow, he **will be landing** on the moon.
When you wake up tomorrow, it **will be landing** on the moon.
When you wake up tomorrow, Andrea **will be landing** on the moon.
When you wake up tomorrow, Urison **will be landing** on the moon.
When you wake up tomorrow, Urison and Andrea **will be landing** on the moon.
When you wake up tomorrow, my cat **will be landing** on the moon.

When the book publishes tomorrow, I **will be listening** to audiobooks.
When the book publishes tomorrow, you **will be listening** to audiobooks.
When the book publishes tomorrow, we **will be listening** to audiobooks.
When the book publishes tomorrow, they **will be listening** to

audiobooks..

When the book publishes tomorrow, he **will be listening** to audiobooks.

When the book publishes tomorrow, she **will be listening** to audiobooks.

When the book publishes tomorrow, it **will be listening** to audiobooks.

When the book publishes tomorrow, Andrea **will be listening** to audiobooks.

When the book publishes tomorrow, Urison **will be listening** to audiobooks.

When the book publishes tomorrow, Andrea and Urison **will be listening** to audiobooks.

When the book publishes tomorrow, my cat **will be listening** to audiobooks.

When I wake up at seven, I **will be getting** a gift.

When you wake up at seven, you **will be getting** a gift.

When we wake up at seven, we **will be getting** a gift.

When they wake up at seven, they **will be getting** a gift.

When he wakes up at seven, he **will be getting** a gift.

When she wakes up at seven, she **will be getting** a gift.

When it wakes up at seven, it **will be getting** a gift.

When Andrea wakes up at seven, she **will be getting** a gift.

When Urison wakes up at seven, he **will be getting** a gift.

When Andrea and Urison wake up at seven, they **will be getting** a gift.

When my cat wakes up at seven, it **will be getting** a gift.

A week from now, I **will be playing** the new game.

A week from now, you **will be playing** the new game.

A week from now, we **will be playing** the new game.

A week from now, they **will be playing** the new game.

A week from now, he **will be playing** the new game.

A week from now, she **will be playing** the new game.

A week from now, it **will be playing** the new game.

A week from now, Andrea **will be playing** the new game.

A week from now, Urison **will be playing** the new game.

A week from now, Andrea and Urison **will be playing** the new

game.
A week from now, my cat **will be playing** the new game.

In a month, I **will be enjoying** life.
In a month, you **will be enjoying** life.
In a month, we **will be enjoying** life.
In a month, they **will be enjoying** life.
In a month, he **will be enjoying** life.
In a month, she **will be enjoying** life.
In a month, it **will be enjoying** life.
In a month, Andrea **will be enjoying** life.
In a month, Urison **will be enjoying** life.
In a month, Andrea and Urison **will be enjoying** life.
In a month, my cat **will be enjoying** life.

When you arrive next week, I **will be surveying**.
When you arrive next week, you **will be surveying**.
When you arrive next week, we **will be surveying**.
When you arrive next week, they **will be surveying**.
When you arrive next week, he **will be surveying**.
When you arrive next week, she **will be surveying**.
When you arrive next week, it **will be surveying**.
When you arrive next week, Andrea **will be surveying**.
When you arrive next week, Urison **will be surveying**.
When you arrive next week, Andrea and Urison **will be surveying**.
When you arrive next week, my cat **will be surveying**.

When the snow comes, I **will be studying**.
When the snow comes, you **will be studying**.
When the snow comes, we **will be studying**.
When the snow comes, they **will be studying**.
When the snow comes, he **will be studying**.
When the snow comes, she **will be studying**.
When the snow comes, it **will be studying**.
When the snow comes, Andrea **will be studying**.
When the snow comes, Urison **will be studying**.
When the snow comes, Andrea and Urison **will be studying**.
When the snow comes, my cat **will be studying**.

Usa questi esercizi per fare ulteriore pratica:

I will be staying home tomorrow.
You will be staying home tomorrow.
We will be staying home tomorrow.
They will be staying home tomorrow.
He will be staying home tomorrow.
She will be staying home tomorrow.
It will be staying home tomorrow.
Andrea will be staying home tomorrow.
Urison will be staying home tomorrow.
Andrea and Urison will be staying home tomorrow.
My cat will be staying home tomorrow.

Next week, I will be buying lunch for a week.
Next week, you will be buying lunch for a week.
Next week, we will be buying lunch for a week.
Next week, they will be buying lunch for a week.
Next week, he will be buying lunch for a week.
Next week, she will be buying lunch for a week.
Next week, it will be buying lunch for a week.
Next week, Andrea will be buying lunch for a week.
Next week, Urison will be buying lunch for a week.
Next week, Andrea and Urison will be buying lunch for a week.
Next week, my cat will be buying lunch for a week.

I will be going to party tonight.
You will be going to party tonight.
We will be going to party tonight.
They will be going to party tonight.
He will be going to party tonight.
She will be going to party tonight.
It will be going to party tonight.
Andrea will be going to party tonight.
Urison will be going to party tonight.
Andrea and Urison will be going to party tonight.
My cat will be going to party tonight.

I will be flying tomorrow.

You will be flying tomorrow.
We will be flying tomorrow.
They will be flying tomorrow.
He will be flying tomorrow.
She will be flying tomorrow.
It will be flying tomorrow.
Andrea will be flying tomorrow.
Urison will be flying tomorrow.
Andrea and Urison will be flying tomorrow.
My cat will be flying tomorrow.

I will be teaching English when I get there.
You will be teaching English when you get there.
We will be teaching English when we get there.
They will be teaching English when they get there.
He will be teaching English when he gets there.
She will be teaching English when she gets there.
It will be teaching English when it gets there.
Andrea will be teaching English when she gets there.
Urison will be teaching English when he gets there.
Andrea and Urison will be teaching English when they get there.
My cat will be teaching English when it gets there.

I will be watching the sky tonight.
You will be watching the sky tonight.
We will be watching the sky tonight.
They will be watching the sky tonight.
He will be watching the sky tonight.
She will be watching the sky tonight.
It will be watching the sky tonight.
Andrea will be watching the sky tonight.
Urison will be watching the sky tonight.
Andrea and Urison will be watching the sky tonight.
My cat will be watching the sky tonight.

In October, I will be munching apples.
In October, you will be munching apples.
In October, we will be munching apples.
In October, they will be munching apples.

In October, he will be munching apples.
In October, she will be munching apples.
In October, it will be munching apples.
In October, Andrea will be munching apples.
In October, Urison will be munching apples.
In October, Andrea and Urison will be munching apples.
In October, my cat will be munching apples.

This summer, I will be washing the marsh.
This summer, you will be washing the marsh.
This summer, we will be washing the marsh.
This summer, they will be washing the marsh.
This summer, he will be washing the marsh.
This summer, she will be washing the marsh.
This summer, it will be washing the marsh.
This summer, Andrea will be washing the marsh.
This summer, Urison will be washing the marsh.
This summer, Andrea and Urison will be washing the marsh.
This summer, my cat will be washing the marsh.

At noon, I will be pushing the bush
At noon, you will be pushing the bush.
At noon, we will be pushing the bush.
At noon, they will be pushing the bush.
At noon, he will be pushing the bush.
At noon, she will be pushing the bush.
At noon, it will be pushing the bush.
At noon, Andrea will be pushing the bush.
At noon, Urison will be pushing the bush.
At noon, Andrea and Urison will be pushing the bush.
At noon, my cat will be pushing the bush.

I will be crossing the crossroad when you stop.
You will be crossing the crossroad when I stop.
We will be crossing the crossroad when you stop.
They will be crossing the crossroad when you stop.
He will be crossing the crossroad when you stop.
She will be crossing the crossroad when you stop.
It will be crossing the crossroad when you stop.

Andrea will be crossing the crossroad when you stop.
Urison will be crossing the crossroad when you stop.
Andrea and Urison will be crossing the crossroad when you stop.
My cat will be crossing the crossroad when you stop.

I will be buzzing along the runway when you land.
You will be buzzing along the runway when I land.
We will be buzzing along the runway when you land.
They will be buzzing along the runway when you land.
He will be buzzing along the runway when you land.
She will be buzzing along the runway when you land.
It will be buzzing along the runway when you land.
Andrea will be buzzing along the runway when you land.
Urison will be buzzing along the runway when you land.
Andrea and Urison will be buzzing along the runway when you land.
My cat will be buzzing along the runway when you land.

I will be jazzing today when Nathan arrives.
You will be jazzing today when Nathan arrives.
We will be jazzing today when Nathan arrives.
They will be jazzing today when Nathan arrives.
He will be jazzing today when Nathan arrives.
She will be jazzing today when Nathan arrives.
It will be jazzing today when Nathan arrives.
Andrea will be jazzing today when Nathan arrives.
Urison will be jazzing today when Nathan arrives.
Andrea and Urison will be jazzing today when Nathan arrives.
My cat will be jazzing today when Nathan arrives.

I will be boxing my boxes before vacation.
You will be boxing my boxes before vacation.
We will be boxing my boxes before vacation.
They will be boxing my boxes before vacation.
He will be boxing my boxes before vacation.
She will be boxing my boxes before vacation.
It will be boxing my boxes before vacation.
Andrea will be boxing my boxes before vacation.
Urison will be boxing my boxes before vacation.

Andrea and Urison will be boxing my boxes before vacation.
My cat will be boxing my boxes before vacation.

I will be relaxing on my relaxation bench at 5:30.
You will be relaxing on my relaxation bench at 5:30.
We will be relaxing on my relaxation bench at 5:30.
They will be relaxing on my relaxation bench at 5:30.
He will be relaxing on my relaxation bench at 5:30.
She will be relaxing on my relaxation bench at 5:30.
It will be relaxing on my relaxation bench at 5:30.
Andrea will be relaxing on my relaxation bench at 5:30.
Urison will be relaxing on my relaxation bench at 5:30.
Andrea and Urison will be relaxing on my relaxation bench at 5:30.
My cat will be relaxing on my relaxation bench at 5:30.

I will be fixing my friend's car while my friend watches.
You will be fixing my friend's car while my friend watches.
We will be fixing my friend's car while my friend watches.
They will be fixing my friend's car while my friend watches.
He will be fixing my friend's car while my friend watches.
She will be fixing my friend's car while my friend watches.
It will be fixing my friend's car while my friend watches.
Andrea will be fixing my friend's car while my friend watches.
Urison will be fixing my friend's car while my friend watches.
Andrea and Urison will be fixing my friend's car while my friend watches.
My cat will be fixing my friend's car while my friend watches.

I will be doing my work while others go to lunch.
You will be doing your work while others go to lunch.
We will be doing our work while others go to lunch.
They will be doing their work while others go to lunch.
He will be doing his work while others go to lunch.
She will be doing her work while others go to lunch.
It will be doing its work while others go to lunch.
Andrea will be doing her work while others go to lunch.
Urison will be doing his work while others go to lunch.
Andrea and Urison will be doing their work while others go to

lunch.
My cat will be doing its work while others go to lunch.

I will be going to work when the sun rises.
You will be going to work when the sun rises.
We will be going to work when the sun rises.
They will be going to work when the sun rises.
He will be going to work when the sun rises.
She will be going to work when the sun rises.
It will be going to work when the sun rises.
Andrea will be going to work when the sun rises.
Urison will be going to work when the sun rises.
Andrea and Urison will be going to work when the sun rises.
My cat will be going to work when the sun rises.

A week from now, I will be having fun on the beach.
A week from now, you will be having fun on the beach.
A week from now, we will be having fun on the beach.
A week from now, they will be having fun on the beach.
A week from now, he will be having fun on the beach.
A week from now, she will be having fun on the beach.
A week from now, it will be having fun on the beach.
A week from now, Andrea will be having fun on the beach.
A week from now, Urison will be having fun on the beach.
A week from now, Andrea and Urison will be having fun on the
beach.
A week from now, my cat will be having fun on the beach.

Ecco altri esercizi:

When the monks come, I will be having vegetables for dinner.
When the monks come, you will be having vegetables for dinner.
When the monks come, we will be having vegetables for dinner.
When the monks come, they will be having vegetables for dinner.
When the monks come, he will be having vegetables for dinner.
When the monks come, she will be having vegetables for dinner.
When the monks come, it will be having vegetables for dinner.
When the monks come, Andrea will be having vegetables for
dinner.

When the monks come, Urison will be having vegetables for dinner.
When the monks come, Andrea and Urison will be having vegetables for dinner.
When the monks come, my cat will be having vegetables for dinner.

An hour from now, I will still be taking the test.
An hour from now, you will still be taking the test.
An hour from now, we will still be taking the test.
An hour from now, they will still be taking the test.
An hour from now, he will still be taking the test.
An hour from now, she will still be taking the test.
An hour from now, it will still be taking the test.
An hour from now, Andrea will still be taking the test.
An hour from now, Urison will still be taking the test.
An hour from now, Andrea and Urison will still be taking the test.
An hour from now, my cat will still be taking the test.

Tonight at 10, I will still be singing at the show.
Tonight at 10, you will still be singing at the show.
Tonight at 10, we will still be singing at the show.
Tonight at 10, they will still be singing at the show.
Tonight at 10, he will still be singing at the show.
Tonight at 10, she will still be singing at the show.
Tonight at 10, it will still be singing at the show.
Tonight at 10, Andrea will still be singing at the show.
Tonight at 10, Urison will still be singing at the show.
Tonight at 10, Andrea and Urison will still be singing at the show.
Tonight at 10, my cat will still be singing at the show.

I will be getting my driver's license soon.
You will be getting your driver's license soon.
We will be getting our driver's license soon.
They will be getting their driver's license soon.
He will be getting his driver's license soon.
She will be getting her driver's license soon.
It will be getting its driver's license soon.
Andrea will be getting her driver's license soon.

Urison will be getting his driver's license soon.
Andrea and Urison will be getting their driver's license soon.
My cat will be getting its driver's license soon.

I will be getting an A on the test.
You will be getting an A on the test.
We will be getting an A on the test.
They will be getting an A on the test.
He will be getting an A on the test.
She will be getting an A on the test.
It will be getting an A on the test.
Andrea will be getting an A on the test.
Urison will be getting an A on the test.
Andrea and Urison will be getting an A on the test.
My cat will be getting an A on the test.

Will I be driving this car?
Will you be driving this car?
Will we be driving this car?
Will they be driving this car?
Will she be driving this car?
Will he be driving this car?
Will it be driving this car?
Will Andrea be driving this car?
Will Urison be driving this car?
Will Andrea and Urison be driving this car?
Will my cat be driving this car?

Will I be picking that up on the way home?
Will you be picking that up on the way home?
Will we be picking that up on the way home?
Will they be picking that up on the way home?
Will she be picking that up on the way home?
Will he be picking that up on the way home?
Will it be picking that up on the way home?
Will Andrea be picking that up on the way home?
Will Urison be picking that up on the way home?
Will Andrea and Urison be picking that up on the way home?
Will my cat be picking that up on the way home?

4.3 Future Perfect Continuous

Osserva la frase seguente:

Tomorrow at this time, I **will have been studying** for 12 hours.

Questo esempio indica che "studying" è un'azione continua che sta attualmente accadendo e continuerà ad accadere fino a domani a quest'ora.

Usiamo il future perfect continuous per riferirci ad azioni o eventi continui che saranno stati completati in un momento specifico del futuro:

- When you come at 10, I **will have been taking** the test for an hour.
- Tomorrow at eight, we **will have been sleeping** for 10 hours.
- By Friday, I **will have been teaching** grammar at the conference for a week.
- When the show is over, they **will have been singing** for 2 hours.

Diamo un'occhiata a questa frase:

When we wake up at eight, we **will have been sleeping** for 10 hours.

Se cambiamo il soggetto in *she*, la frase avrà questo aspetto:

When she wakes up at eight, she **will have been sleeping** for 10 hours.

Ora impariamo il future perfect continuous:

By eight o'clock, I **will have been listening** to audiobooks for two hours.
By eight o'clock, you **will have been listening** to audiobooks for two hours.

117

By eight o'clock, we **will have been listening** to audiobooks for two hours.

By eight o'clock, they **will have been listening** to audiobooks for two hours..

By eight o'clock, he **will have been listening** to audiobooks for two hours.

By eight o'clock, she **will have been listening** to audiobooks for two hours.

By eight o'clock, it **will have been listening** to audiobooks for two hours.

By eight o'clock, Andrea **will have been listening** to audiobooks for two hours.

By eight o'clock, Urison **will have been listening** to audiobooks for two hours.

By eight o'clock, Andrea and Urison **will have been listening** to audiobooks for two hours.

By eight o'clock, my cat **will have been listening** to audiobooks for two hours.

In two days, I **will have been learning** the tenses for two weeks.

In two days, you **will have been learning** the tenses for two weeks.

In two days, we **will have been learning** the tenses for two weeks.

In two days, they **will have been learning** the tenses for two weeks.

In two days, he **will have been learning** the tenses for two weeks.

In two days, she **will have been learning** the tenses for two weeks.

In two days, it **will have been learning** the tenses for two weeks.

In two days, Andrea **will have been learning** the tenses for two weeks.

In two days, Urison **will have been learning** the tenses for two weeks.

In two days, Andrea and Urison **will have been learning** the tenses for two weeks.

In two days, my cat **will have been learning** the tenses for two weeks.

A week from now, I **will have been playing** the new game for a month.

A week from now, you **will have been playing** the new game for a month.

A week from now, we **will have been playing** the new game for a month.

A week from now, they **will have been playing** the new game for a month.

A week from now, he **will have been playing** the new game for a month.

A week from now, she **will have been playing** the new game for a month.

A week from now, it **will have been playing** the new game for a month.

A week from now, Andrea **will have been playing** the new game for a month.

A week from now, Urison **will have been playing** the new game for a month.

A week from now, Andrea and Urison **will have been playing** the new game for a month.

A week from now, my cat **will have been playing** the new game for a month.

In a month, I **will have been enjoying** life for a year.
In a month, you **will have been enjoying** life for a year.
In a month, we **will have been enjoying** life for a year.
In a month, they **will have been enjoying** life for a year.
In a month, he **will have been enjoying** life for a year.
In a month, she **will have been enjoying** life for a year.
In a month, it **will have been enjoying** life for a year.
In a month, Andrea **will have been enjoying** life for a year.
In a month, Urison **will have been enjoying** life for a year.
In a month, Andrea and Urison **will have been enjoying** life for a year.
In a month, my cat **will have been enjoying** life for a year.

When you arrive next week, I **will have been surveying** for three weeks.

When you arrive next week, you **will have been surveying** for three weeks.

When you arrive next week, we **will have been surveying** for three weeks.

When you arrive next week, they **will have been surveying** for three weeks.

When you arrive next week, he **will have been surveying** for three weeks.

When you arrive next week, she **will have been surveying** for three weeks.

When you arrive next week, it **will have been surveying** for three weeks.

When you arrive next week, Andrea **will have been surveying** for three weeks.

When you arrive next week, Urison **will have been surveying** for three weeks.

When you arrive next week, Andrea and Urison **will have been surveying** for three weeks.

When you arrive next week, my cat **will have been surveying** for three weeks.

When the snow stops, I **will have been playing** for two hours.

When the snow stops, you **will have been playing** for two hours.

When the snow stops, we **will have been playing** for two hours.

When the snow stops, they **will have been playing** for two hours.

When the snow stops, he **will have been playing** for two hours.

When the snow stops, she **will have been playing** for two hours.

When the snow stops, it **will have been playing** for two hours.

When the snow stops, Andrea **will have been playing** for two hours.

When the snow stops, Urison **will have been playing** for two hours.

When the snow stops, Andrea and Urison **will have been playing** for two hours.

When the snow stops, my cat **will have been playing** for two hours.

Acquisiamo il future perfect continuous nel nostro subconscio. Continuiamo ad esercitarci:

When the snow melts, I **will have been staying** home for a week.

When the snow melts, you **will have been staying** home for a

week.
When the snow melts, we **will have been staying** home for a week.
When the snow melts, they **will have been staying** home for a week.
When the snow melts, he **will have been staying** home for a week.
When the snow melts, she **will have been staying** home for a week.
When the snow melts, it **will have been staying** home for a week.
When the snow melts, Andrea **will have been staying** home for a week.
When the snow melts, Urison **will have been staying** home for a week.
When the snow melts, Andrea and Urison **will have been staying** home for a week.
When the snow melts, my cat **will have been staying** home for a week.

By tomorrow, I **will have been buying** lunch for a week.
By tomorrow, you **will have been buying** lunch for a week.
By tomorrow, we **will have been buying** lunch for a week.
By tomorrow, they **will have been buying** lunch for a week.
By tomorrow, he **will have been buying** lunch for a week.
By tomorrow, she **will have been buying** lunch for a week.
By tomorrow, it **will have been buying** lunch for a week.
By tomorrow, Andrea **will have been buying** lunch for a week.
By tomorrow, Urison **will have been buying** lunch for a week.
By tomorrow, Andrea and Urison **will have been buying** lunch for a week.
By tomorrow, my cat **will have been buying** lunch for a week.

When the plane lands, I **will have been flying** for 3000 hours.
When the plane lands, you **will have been flying** for 3000 hours.
When the plane lands, we **will have been flying** for 3000 hours.
When the plane lands, they **will have been flying** for 3000 hours.
When the plane lands, he **will have been flying** for 3000 hours.
When the plane lands, she **will have been flying** for 3000 hours.
When the plane lands, it **will have been flying** for 3000 hours.
When the plane lands, Andrea **will have been flying** for 3000

hours.

When the plane lands, Urison **will have been flying** for 3000 hours.

When the plane lands, Andrea and Urison **will have been flying** for 3000 hours.

When the plane lands, my cat **will have been flying** for 3000 hours.

When the class ends, I **will have been teaching** English for three hours.

When the class ends, you **will have been teaching** English for three hours.

When the class ends, we **will have been teaching** English for three hours.

When the class ends, they **will have been teaching** English for three hours.

When the class ends, he **will have been teaching** English for three hours.

When the class ends, she **will have been teaching** English for three hours.

When the class ends, it **will have been teaching** English for three hours.

When the class ends, Andrea **will have been teaching** English for three hours.

When the class ends, Urison **will have been teaching** English for three hours.

When the class ends, Andrea and Urison **will have been teaching** English for three hours.

When the class ends, my cat **will have been teaching** English for three hours.

When the cloud moves in, I **will have been watching** the night sky for four hours.

When the cloud moves in, you **will have been watching** the night sky for four hours.

When the cloud moves in, we **will have been watching** the night sky for four hours.

When the cloud moves in, they **will have been watching** the night sky for four hours.

When the cloud moves in, he **will have been watching** the night sky for four hours.

When the cloud moves in, she **will have been watching** the night sky for four hours.

When the cloud moves in, it **will have been watching** the night sky for four hours.

When the cloud moves in, Andrea **will have been watching** the night sky for four hours.

When the cloud moves in, Urison **will have been watching** the night sky for four hours.

When the cloud moves in, Andrea and Urison **will have been watching** the night sky for four hours.

When the cloud moves in, my cat **will have been watching** the night sky for four hours.

In October, I **will have been munching** apples for a month.

In October, you **will have been munching** apples for a month.

In October, we **will have been munching** apples for a month.

In October, they **will have been munching** apples for a month.

In October, he **will have been munching** apples for a month.

In October, she **will have been munching** apples for a month.

In October, it **will have been munching** apples for a month.

In October, Andrea **will have been munching** apples for a month.

In October, Urison **will have been munching** apples for a month.

In October, Andrea and Urison **will have been munching** apples for a month.

In October, my cat **will have been munching** apples for a month.

By September, I **will have been washing** the marsh for three months.

By September, you **will have been washing** the marsh for three months.

By September, we **will have been washing** the marsh for three months.

By September, they **will have been washing** the marsh for three months.

By September, he **will have been washing** the marsh for three months.

By September, she **will have been washing** the marsh for three months.

By September, it **will have been washing** the marsh for three months.

By September, Andrea **will have been washing** the marsh for three months.

By September, Urison **will have been washing** the marsh for three months.

By September, Andrea and Urison **will have been washing** the marsh for three months.

By September, my cat **will have been washing** the marsh for three months.

At noon, I **will have been pushing** the bush for an hour

At noon, you **will have been pushing** the bush for an hour.

At noon, we **will have been pushing** the bush for an hour.

At noon, they **will have been pushing** the bush for an hour.

At noon, he **will have been pushing** the bush for an hour.

At noon, she **will have been pushing** the bush for an hour.

At noon, it **will have been pushing** the bush for an hour.

At noon, Andrea **will have been pushing** the bush for an hour.

At noon, Urison **will have been pushing** the bush for an hour.

At noon, Andrea and Urison **will have been pushing** the bush for an hour.

At noon, my cat **will have been pushing** the bush for an hour.

I **will have been buzzing** along the runway for 30 minutes when you land.

You **will have been buzzing** along the runway for 30 minutes when you land.

We **will have been buzzing** along the runway for 30 minutes when you land.

They **will have been buzzing** along the runway for 30 minutes when you land.

He **will have been buzzing** along the runway for 30 minutes when you land.

She **will have been buzzing** along the runway for 30 minutes when you land.

It **will have been buzzing** along the runway for 30 minutes when you land.

Andrea **will have been buzzing** along the runway for 30 minutes when you land.

Urison **will have been buzzing** along the runway for 30 minutes when you land.

Andrea and Urison **will have been buzzing** along the runway for 30 minutes when you land.

My cat **will have been buzzing** along the runway for 30 minutes when you land.

I **will have been jazzing** for two hours when Nathan arrives.

You **will have been jazzing** for two hours when Nathan arrives.

We **will have been jazzing** for two hours when Nathan arrives.

They **will have been jazzing** for two hours when Nathan arrives.

He **will have been jazzing** for two hours when Nathan arrives.

She **will have been jazzing** for two hours when Nathan arrives.

It **will have been jazzing** for two hours when Nathan arrives.

Andrea **will have been jazzing** for two hours when Nathan arrives.

Urison **will have been jazzing** for two hours when Nathan arrives.

Andrea and Urison **will have been jazzing** for two hours when Nathan arrives.

My cat **will have been jazzing** for two hours when Nathan arrives.

I **will have been boxing** my boxes for three days when the day comes.

You **will have been boxing** my boxes for three days when the day comes.

We **will have been boxing** my boxes for three days when the day comes.

They **will have been boxing** my boxes for three days when the day comes.

He **will have been boxing** my boxes for three days when the day comes.

She **will have been boxing** my boxes for three days when the day comes.

It **will have been boxing** my boxes for three days when the day comes.

Andrea **will have been boxing** my boxes for three days when the day comes.

Urison **will have been boxing** my boxes for three days when the day comes.

Andrea and Urison will have been boxing my boxes for three days when the day comes.

My cat will have been boxing my boxes for three days when the day comes.

By noon, I will have been relaxing on my relaxation bench for two hours

By noon, you will have been relaxing on my relaxation bench for two hours.

By noon, we will have been relaxing on my relaxation bench for two hours.

By noon, they will have been relaxing on my relaxation bench for two hours.

By noon, he will have been relaxing on my relaxation bench for two hours.

By noon, she will have been relaxing on my relaxation bench for two hours.

By noon, it will have been relaxing on my relaxation bench for two hours.

By noon, Andrea will have been relaxing on my relaxation bench for two hours.

By noon, Urison will have been relaxing on my relaxation bench for two hours.

By noon, Andrea and Urison will have been relaxing on my relaxation bench for two hours.

By noon, my cat will have been relaxing on my relaxation bench for two hours.

By 11, I will have been fixing my friend's car for three hours

By 11, you will have been fixing my friend's car for three hours.

By 11, we will have been fixing my friend's car for three hours.

By 11, they will have been fixing my friend's car for three hours.

By 11, he will have been fixing my friend's car for three hours.

By 11, she will have been fixing my friend's car for three hours.

By 11, it will have been fixing my friend's car for three hours.

By 11, Andrea will have been fixing my friend's car for three hours.

By 11, Urison will have been fixing my friend's car for three hours.

By 11, Andrea and Urison will have been fixing my friend's car for three hours.

By 11, my cat will have been fixing my friend's car for three hours.

I will have been doing my work for six hours when others go to lunch.

You will have been doing your work for six hours when others go to lunch.

We will have been doing our work for six hours when others go to lunch.

They will have been doing their work for six hours when others go to lunch.

He will have been doing his work for six hours when others go to lunch.

She will have been doing her work for six hours when others go to lunch.

It will have been doing its work for six hours when others go to lunch.

Andrea will have been doing her work for six hours when others go to lunch.

Urison will have been doing his work for six hours when others go to lunch.

Andrea and Urison will have been doing their work for six hours when others go to lunch.

My cat will have been doing its work for six hours when others go to lunch.

I will have been going to work for 10 minutes when the sun rises.

You will have been going to work for 10 minutes when the sun rises.

We will have been going to work for 10 minutes when the sun rises.

They will have been going to work for 10 minutes when the sun rises.

He will have been going to work for 10 minutes when the sun rises.

She will have been going to work for 10 minutes when the sun rises.

It **will have been going** to work for 10 minutes when the sun rises.

Andrea **will have been going** to work for 10 minutes when the sun rises.

Urison **will have been going** to work for 10 minutes when the sun rises.

Andrea and Urison **will have been going** to work for 10 minutes when the sun rises.

My cat **will have been going** to work for 10 minutes when the sun rises.

4.4 Future Perfect

Osserva il seguente esempio:

I **will have studied** all 12 tenses by the time I finish this chapter.

Usiamo il future perfect per riferirci ad azioni o eventi continui che saranno completati in un determinato periodo di tempo nel futuro:
- By the time you arrive, I **will have taken** the test.
- By next year, we **will have worked** here for 10 years.
- I **will have taught** grammar at the conference for a month by next week.
- They **will have finished** the work by the end of the month.

Dai un'occhiata a questa frase:

By the time we wake up, we **will have slept** for 10 hours.

Ora, se cambiamo il soggetto in *she*, tutto il resto rimane invariato:

By the time she wakes up, she **will have slept** for 10 hours.

Adesso impariamo il future perfect:

By the end of this hour, I **will have listened** to audiobooks for two hours.
By the end of this hour, you **will have listened** to audiobooks for two hours.
By the end of this hour, we **will have listened** to audiobooks for two hours.
By the end of this hour, they **will have listened** to audiobooks for two hours.
By the end of this hour, he **will have listened** to audiobooks for two hours.
By the end of this hour, she **will have listened** to audiobooks for two hours.
By the end of this hour, it **will have listened** to audiobooks for two hours.

By the end of this hour, Andrea **will have listened** to audiobooks for two hours.

By the end of this hour, Urison **will have listened** to audiobooks for two hours.

By the end of this hour, Andrea and Urison **will have listened** to audiobooks for two hours.

By the end of this hour, my cat **will have listened** to audiobooks for two hours.

By the end of the week, I **will have learned** tenses for two weeks.

By the end of the week, you **will have learned** tenses for two weeks.

By the end of the week, we **will have learned** tenses for two weeks.

By the end of the week, they **will have learned** tenses for two weeks.

By the end of the week, he **will have learned** tenses for two weeks.

By the end of the week, she **will have learned** tenses for two weeks.

By the end of the week, it **will have learned** tenses for two weeks.

By the end of the week, Andrea **will have learned** tenses for two weeks.

By the end of the week, Urison **will have learned** tenses for two weeks.

By the end of the week, Andrea and Urison **will have learned** tenses for two weeks.

By the end of the week, my cat **will have learned** tenses for two weeks.

By the end of the month, I **will have enjoyed** life for a year.

By the end of the month, you **will have enjoyed** life for a year.

By the end of the month, we **will have enjoyed** life for a year.

By the end of the month, they **will have enjoyed** life for a year.

By the end of the month, he **will have enjoyed** life for a year.

By the end of the month, she **will have enjoyed** life for a year.

By the end of the month, it **will have enjoyed** life for a year.

By the end of the month, Andrea **will have enjoyed** life for a year.

By the end of the month, Urison **will have enjoyed** life for a year.

By the end of the month, Andrea and Urison will have enjoyed life for a year.
By the end of the month, my cat will have enjoyed life for a year.

By the time you arrive, I will have surveyed for three weeks.
By the time I arrive, you will have surveyed for three weeks.
By the time you arrive, we will have surveyed for three weeks.
By the time you arrive, they will have surveyed for three weeks.
By the time you arrive, he will have surveyed for three weeks.
By the time you arrive, she will have surveyed for three weeks.
By the time you arrive, it will have surveyed for three weeks.
By the time you arrive, Andrea will have surveyed for three weeks.
By the time you arrive, Urison will have surveyed for three weeks.
By the time you arrive, Andrea and Urison will have surveyed for three weeks.
By the time you arrive, my cat will have surveyed for three weeks.

Ora che conosci il future perfect, esegui i seguenti esercizi per farlo entrare nel tuo subconscio:

By the end of the hour, I will have played for two hours.
By the end of the hour, you will have played for two hours.
By the end of the hour, we will have played for two hours.
By the end of the hour, they will have played for two hours.
By the end of the hour, he will have played for two hours.
By the end of the hour, she will have played for two hours.
By the end of the hour, it will have played for two hours.
By the end of the hour, Andrea will have played for two hours.
By the end of the hour, Urison will have played for two hours.
By the end of the hour, Andrea and Urison will have played for two hours.
By the end of the hour, my cat will have played for two hours.

By the time the snow melts, I will have stayed home for a week.
By the time the snow melts, you will have stayed home for a week.
By the time the snow melts, we will have stayed home for a week.

By the time the snow melts, they will have stayed home for a week.
By the time the snow melts, he will have stayed home for a week.
By the time the snow melts, she will have stayed home for a week.
By the time the snow melts, it will have stayed home for a week.
By the time the snow melts, Andrea will have stayed home for a week.
By the time the snow melts, Urison will have stayed home for a week.
By the time the snow melts, Andrea and Urison will have stayed home for a week.
By the time the snow melts, my cat will have stayed home for a week.

By tomorrow, I will have bought lunch for a week.
By tomorrow, you will have bought lunch for a week.
By tomorrow, we will have bought lunch for a week.
By tomorrow, they will have bought lunch for a week.
By tomorrow, he will have bought lunch for a week.
By tomorrow, she will have bought lunch for a week.
By tomorrow, it will have bought lunch for a week.
By tomorrow, Andrea will have bought lunch for a week.
By tomorrow, Urison will have bought lunch for a week.
By tomorrow, Andrea and Urison will have bought lunch for a week.
By tomorrow, my cat will have bought lunch for a week.

By the time the plane lands, I will have flown for 3000 hours.
By the time the plane lands, you will have flown for 3000 hours.
By the time the plane lands, we will have flown for 3000 hours.
By the time the plane lands, they will have flown for 3000 hours.
By the time the plane lands, he will have flown for 3000 hours.
By the time the plane lands, she will have flown for 3000 hours.
By the time the plane lands, it will have flown for 3000 hours.
By the time the plane lands, Andrea will have flown for 3000 hours.
By the time the plane lands, Urison will have flown for 3000 hours.
By the time the plane lands, Andrea and Urison will have flown

for 3000 hours.
By the time the plane lands, my cat **will have flown** for 3000 hours.

At the end of the class, I **will have taught** English for three hours.
At the end of the class, you **will have taught** English for three hours.
At the end of the class, we **will have taught** English for three hours.
At the end of the class, they **will have taught** English for three hours.
At the end of the class, he **will have taught** English for three hours.
At the end of the class, she **will have taught** English for three hours.
At the end of the class, it **will have taught** English for three hours.
At the end of the class, Andrea **will have taught** English for three hours.
At the end of the class, Urison **will have taught** English for three hours.
At the end of the class, Andrea and Urison **will have taught** English for three hours.
At the end of the class, my cat **will have taught** English for three hours.

By the time the cloud moves in, I **will have watched** the night sky for four hours.
By the time the cloud moves in, you **will have watched** the night sky for four hours.
By the time the cloud moves in, we **will have watched** the night sky for four hours.
By the time the cloud moves in, they **will have watched** the night sky for four hours.
By the time the cloud moves in, he **will have watched** the night sky for four hours.
By the time the cloud moves in, she **will have watched** the night sky for four hours.
By the time the cloud moves in, it **will have watched** the night sky for four hours.

By the time the cloud moves in, Andrea **will have watched** the night sky for four hours.
By the time the cloud moves in, Urison **will have watched** the night sky for four hours.
By the time the cloud moves in, Andrea and Urison **will have watched** the night sky for four hours.
By the time the cloud moves in, my cat **will have watched** the night sky for four hours.

In October, I **will have munched** apples for a month.
In October, you **will have munched** apples for a month.
In October, we **will have munched** apples for a month.
In October, they **will have munched** apples for a month.
In October, he **will have munched** apples for a month.
In October, she **will have munched** apples for a month.
In October, it **will have munched** apples for a month.
In October, Andrea **will have munched** apples for a month.
In October, Urison **will have munched** apples for a month.
In October, Andrea and Urison **will have munched** apples for a month.
In October, my cat **will have munched** apples for a month.

By September, I **will have washed** the marsh for three months.
By September, you **will have washed** the marsh for three months.
By September, we **will have washed** the marsh for three months.
By September, they **will have washed** the marsh for three months.
By September, he **will have washed** the marsh for three months.
By September, she **will have washed** the marsh for three months.
By September, it **will have washed** the marsh for three months.
By September, Andrea **will have washed** the marsh for three months.
By September, Urison **will have washed** the marsh for three months.
By September, Andrea and Urison **will have washed** the marsh for three months.
By September, my cat **will have washed** the marsh for three months.

By noon, I **will have pushed** the bush for an hour

By noon, you will have pushed the bush for an hour.
By noon, we will have pushed the bush for an hour.
By noon, they will have pushed the bush for an hour.
By noon, he will have pushed the bush for an hour.
By noon, she will have pushed the bush for an hour.
By noon, it will have pushed the bush for an hour.
By noon, Andrea will have pushed the bush for an hour.
By noon, Urison will have pushed the bush for an hour.
By noon, Andrea and Urison will have pushed the bush for an hour.
By noon, my cat will have pushed the bush for an hour.

I will have buzzed along the runway for 30 minutes when you land.
You will have buzzed along the runway for 30 minutes when I land.
We will have buzzed along the runway for 30 minutes when you land.
They will have buzzed along the runway for 30 minutes when you land.
He will have buzzed along the runway for 30 minutes when you land.
She will have buzzed along the runway for 30 minutes when you land.
It will have buzzed along the runway for 30 minutes when you land.
Andrea will have buzzed along the runway for 30 minutes when you land.
Urison will have buzzed along the runway for 30 minutes when you land.
Andrea and Urison will have buzzed along the runway for 30 minutes when you land.
My cat will have buzzed along the runway for 30 minutes when you land.

I will have jazzed for two hours when Nathan arrives.
You will have jazzed for two hours when Nathan arrives.
We will have jazzed for two hours when Nathan arrives.
They will have jazzed for two hours when Nathan arrives.

He **will have jazzed** for two hours when Nathan arrives.
She **will have jazzed** for two hours when Nathan arrives.
It **will have jazzed** for two hours when Nathan arrives.
Andrea **will have jazzed** for two hours when Nathan arrives.
Urison **will have jazzed** for two hours when Nathan arrives.
Andrea and Urison **will have jazzed** for two hours when Nathan arrives.
My cat **will have jazzed** for two hours when Nathan arrives.

I **will have boxed** my boxes for three days when Nathan arrives.
You **will have boxed** my boxes for three days when Nathan arrives.
We **will have boxed** my boxes for three days when Nathan arrives.
They **will have boxed** my boxes for three days when Nathan arrives.
He **will have boxed** my boxes for three days when Nathan arrives.
She **will have boxed** my boxes for three days when Nathan arrives.
It **will have boxed** my boxes for three days when Nathan arrives.
Andrea **will have boxed** my boxes for three days when Nathan arrives.
Urison **will have boxed** my boxes for three days when Nathan arrives.
Andrea and Urison **will have boxed** my boxes for three days when Nathan arrives.
My cat **will have boxed** my boxes for three days when Nathan arrives.

By noon, I **will have relaxed** on my relaxation bench for two hours.
By noon, you **will have relaxed** on my relaxation bench for two hours.
By noon, we **will have relaxed** on my relaxation bench for two hours.
By noon, they **will have relaxed** on my relaxation bench for two hours.
By noon, he **will have relaxed** on my relaxation bench for two hours.
By noon, she **will have relaxed** on my relaxation bench for two hours.

By noon, it **will have relaxed** on my relaxation bench for two hours.

By noon, Andrea **will have relaxed** on my relaxation bench for two hours.

By noon, Urison **will have relaxed** on my relaxation bench for two hours.

By noon, Andrea and Urison **will have relaxed** on my relaxation bench for two hours.

By noon, my cat **will have relaxed** on my relaxation bench for two hours.

By noon, I **will have fixed** my friend's car for three hours.
By noon, you **will have fixed** my friend's car for three hours.
By noon, we **will have fixed** my friend's car for three hours.
By noon, they **will have fixed** my friend's car for three hours.
By noon, he **will have fixed** my friend's car for three hours.
By noon, she **will have fixed** my friend's car for three hours.
By noon, it **will have fixed** my friend's car for three hours.
By noon, Andrea **will have fixed** my friend's car for three hours.
By noon, Urison **will have fixed** my friend's car for three hours.
By noon, Andrea and Urison **will have fixed** my friend's car for three hours.
By noon, my cat **will have fixed** my friend's car for three hours.

I **will have done** my work for six hours when others go to lunch.
You **will have done** your work for six hours when others go to lunch.
We **will have done** our work for six hours when others go to lunch.
They **will have done** their work for six hours when others go to lunch.
He **will have done** his work for six hours when others go to lunch.
She **will have done** her work for six hours when others go to lunch.
It **will have done** its work for six hours when others go to lunch.
Andrea **will have done** her work for six hours when others go to lunch.
Urison **will have done** his work for six hours when others go to lunch.
Andrea and Urison **will have done** their work for six hours when

others go to lunch.
My cat **will have done** its work for six hours when others go to lunch.

I **will have gone** to work for 10 minutes when the sun rises.
You **will have gone** to work for 10 minutes when the sun rises.
They **will have gone** to work for 10 minutes when the sun rises.
He **will have gone** to work for 10 minutes when the sun rises.
She **will have gone** to work for 10 minutes when the sun rises.
It **will have gone** to work for 10 minutes when the sun rises.
Andrea **will have gone** to work for 10 minutes when the sun rises.
Urison **will have gone** to work for 10 minutes when the sun rises.
Andrea and Urison **will have gone** to work for 10 minutes when the sun rises.
My cat **will have gone** to work for 10 minutes when the sun rises.

Capitolo 5: Condizionale

- If the sun comes up, the frost **melts**.
- If birds have no wings, they don't **fly**.
- If you throw a rock into a pond, it **creates** ripples.

Queste frasi contengono tutte tempi condizionali su verità generali della natura. Se ciò accade, ciò accade. Nella maggior parte dei casi, usiamo la parola *if* nelle frasi che contengono un paio di clausole condizionali. Usiamo i tempi condizionali per fare ipotesi su cosa potrebbe accadere, cosa potrebbe essere accaduto e cosa vorremmo che accadesse.

Zero Conditional – Indica la realtà e i fatti prevedibili:

Questo condizionale è usato per verità generali ed eventi reali. Lo usiamo per qualcosa che succede sempre nello stesso modo. Lo usiamo quando parliamo di qualcosa con un risultato prevedibile e garantito ogni volta:

- If the sun comes up, the frost **melts**.
- If you throw a rock into a pond, it **creates** ripples.

Questi sono fatti. Succedono sempre. La clausola *if* è in simple present, e anche la clausola principale è in simple present.

- If you throw a ball into the air, it **comes** back down.
- If a meteorite hits the earth, it **creates** a flash.

Anche questi sono fatti. Succedono ogni volta. Quando la situazione è completamente prevedibile, usa il present tense nella clausola *if* e il present tense nella clausola principale.

First Conditional — Indica che qualcosa è irreale, ma possibile:

Questo condizionale è usato per le situazioni irreali ma probabili. Usiamo questo condizionale per qualcosa che non è successo ma che probabilmente accadrà. Se ciò accade, probabilmente quell'altra cosa accadrà.

- If I get 100 on my test, I **will laugh**.

Questo non è ancora successo. Non ho avuto 100 al test. È irreale. Ma è probabile che riderei se ottenessi 100 al test.

Nel First Conditional, usiamo il simple present in situazioni irreali e probabili. Usiamo *will* + *verbo* nella clausola principale.

- If it snows, animals **will hide**.
- If I have a dollar, I **will save** it.
- If they come, we **will play** games.
- If you leave now, you **will get** there on time.

Second Conditional— Indica che qualcosa è irreale e improbabile.

Il second conditional viene utilizzato per situazioni irreali e improbabili. Usiamo questo condizionale per qualcosa che non è successo e che immaginiamo sia improbabile che accada, ad esempio:

- If we threw a rock at a beehive, we **would need** to run to stay alive.

Questo non è ancora successo. Non abbiamo gettato un sasso in un alveare. È irreale. Non crediamo che succederà. È improbabile che buttiamo una pietra in un alveare.

Nel Second Conditional, usiamo il simple past per indicare situazioni irreali e improbabili. Usiamo *would* + *verbo* nella clausola principale:

- If Andrea came yesterday, we **would write** this book together.
- If I *were* rich, I **would live** on an island. (Nel second

conditional, invece di usare **was**, usa **were**.)

- If I lived on an island, I **would fly** to work.
- If humans didn't **play** with fire, humans **would** still **be living** in caves.

Third Conditional— Indica una condizione irreale.

Questo condizionale viene utilizzato per situazioni passat che non si sono verificate. Sono irreali. Immaginiamo solo quali sarebbero state le conseguenze, ad esempio:

- If Andrea had come yesterday, we **would have written** this book together.
- If I had been rich, I **would have lived** on an island.
- If I had lived on an island, I **would have flown** to work.
- If you had gotten 100 on your test, you **would have laughed**.

Nel Third Conditional, utilizziamo il past perfect nella clausola condizionale e *would have* + verbo al participio passato nella clausola principale.

Ora guardiamoli tutti insieme.

0 Conditional	If it snows,	Animals **hide**.
1st Conditional	If it snows,	Animals **will hide**.
2nd Conditional	If it snowed,	Animals **would hide**.
3rd Conditional	If it had snowed,	Animals **would have hidden**.

Capitolo 6: Concordanza soggetto-verbo

In inglese, il soggetto e il verbo devono essere accordati l'uno con l'altro. Guarda questi due esempi per scoprire se sono corretti:
- The cow **moos**.
- The cows **moo**.

Sì. Sono corretti. Nel tempo presente, quando hai un soggetto singolare, aggiungi una *s* alla fine del verbo per accordarlo:
- The kid **jumps**.
- The horse **runs**.
- The planet **revolves** around the sun.

In alternativa, quando hai un soggetto plurale, usa semplicemente il verbo nella sua forma originale:
- The kids **jump**.
- The horses **run**.
- The planets **revolve** around the sun.

Per la terza persona singolare, aggiungi una *s* alla fine del verbo:
- He **succeeds**.
- She **succeeds**.
- It **succeeds**.
- Andrea **succeeds**.
- Urison **succeeds**.

Ed ecco come dovrebbe apparire la tua frase per la prima persona, la seconda persona e la terza persona plurale:
- I **succeed**.
- You **succeed**.
- They **succeed**.
- Andrea and Urison **succeed**.

6.1 Pronomi indefiniti singolari

I pronomi indefiniti possono essere singolari o plurali. Ecco alcuni esempi:

- **Everyone breathes**.
- **Everything begins**.
- **Anything is** possible.

Quando usiamo i pronomi indefiniti singolari, aggiungiamo una *s* alla fine del verbo. Tuffiamoci in:

Anybody
Anybody **gets** it for free.

Anyone
Does anyone **have** an idea?

Anything
Anything **is** possible.

Anywhere
Anywhere **is** a good place.

Each
Each of the football players **is** ready to start the game.

Either
Either of us **is** capable of giving help.

Everybody
Everybody **is** fine.

Everyone
Everyone **has** helped.

Everything
Everything **is** okay.

Everywhere
Everywhere **is** safe.

Little
Little information **is** helpful.

Much
Much time **has been** used in production.

Neither
Neither of them **is** an astronaut.

Nobody
Nobody **wonders** why.

No one
No one **knows** how.

Nothing
Nothing **matters**.

Nowhere
There **is** nowhere that **hasn't been searched**.

One
One person **is** enough.

Somebody
Somebody **has** to do it.

Someone
Someone **is coming**.

Something
Something **is** better than nothing.

Somewhere
Somewhere **is** better than nowhere.

Everything
Everything **has been done**.

Somebody
Somebody **has left** her phone.

Everybody
Everybody **has taken** his chance.

6.2 Pronomi indefiniti plurali

Ecco alcuni esercizi di pronomi indefiniti plurali:

Both
Both Urison and Andrea **are** good at English.

Few
Few **know** the secret.

Fewer
Fewer **know** the truth.

Many
Many **are** the original artists.

Others
Others **are** later comers.

Several
Several **are** students.

6.3 Pronomi indefiniti che possono essere sia singolari che plurali

I seguenti pronomi indefiniti possono essere singolari o plurali:

All
All of the water **is gone**. (All è singolare qui perché stiamo parlando di acqua, che non è numerabile.)
All **are** welcome. (All è plurale qui perché possiamo contare il numero di persone.)

Regola generale: usa questi pronomi indefiniti come singolari quando parli di soggetti non numerabili (come l'acqua). Usa questi pronomi indefiniti come plurali se il soggetto è numerabile (come il numero di persone).

Any
Any of the information **is** helpful.
Any of the computers **are** available.

Either...or
Either Andrea or Urison **is** capable of giving help. (Abbina il verbo alla parola più vicina.)
Either Andrea or her friends **are** capable of giving help.

Neither...nor
Neither Andrea nor Nathan **is** an astronaut.
Neither Andrea nor the players **are** astronauts. (Abbina il verbo alla parola più vicina.)

More
More sugar **is coming**.
More sugar canes **are coming**.
More than half of the sugar **has come**.
More than one sugar cane **has come**. (More than one qui prende il singolare.)
More than half of the sugar canes **have come**. (More than half qui

147

prende il plurale.)

Most
Most of the milk is gone.
Most of the cows are gone.

None
None of the water is potable.
None of the players are astronauts.

Some
Some of the stars are very bright. (Le stelle sono numerabili.)
Some of the heat escapes from the stars. (Il calore non è numerabile.)

Such
Such water is tasty.
Such streams are welcome.

6.4 Sostantivi non numerabili

Ecco alcuni esempi di sostantivi non numerabili:
- water
- money
- sugar
- happiness

I sostantivi non numerabili sono nomi che non possono essere contati. Possiamo avere un bicchiere d'acqua, ma non possiamo avere un'acqua. Possiamo avere $10, ma non possiamo avere 10 soldi.

I sostantivi non numerabili sono sempre singolari. Pertanto, dobbiamo aggiungere una *s* alla fine del verbo:
- Rice **grows** in the fields.
- Knowledge **gives** you power.
- Water **is** also known as H2O.

Esistono decine di migliaia di sostantivi non numerabili. Ecco alcuni di essi elencati per categorie.

Concetti astratti -- Parole che si riferiscono a idee o qualità:
Beauty, confidence, excitement, experience, freedom, fun, happiness, health, information, intelligence, time

Tipi di attività (nella forma in –ing):
Swimming, dancing, reading, laughing, hiking, working, writing, drinking, studying

Cibi:
Milk, corn, salt, flour, rice, wheat, bread, sugar, meat, water

Temi senza una forma definita:
Work, equipment, homework, money, makeup, news, transportation, clothing, postage, trash, luggage, jewelry, traffic

Natura:
Air, darkness, gravity, humidity, heat, ice, light, water, wind, fire, gold, silver, oxygen, sunshine

Campi accademici di studio:
Economics, linguistics, physics, astronomy, biology, music, science, history, statistics, chemistry

Usiamo i quantificatori prima dei sostantivi non numerabili:
- A glass of water
- A loaf of bread
- A lot of information

Alcuni nomi possono essere sia numerabili che non numerabili. Osserviamo alcuni esempi:
- Glass **is** different than plastic.
- Glasses on the table **are filled** with water.

Inoltre:
- Adventure **is** what he likes.
- He **had** two adventures on his last trip.

Capitolo 7: Vista d'insieme

Mettiamo insieme i tempi presente, passato e futuro.

Simple:
They **study** together every Monday.
They **studied** together last Monday.
They **will study** together next Monday.

Continuous:
They **are studying** right now.
They **were studying** together when a UFO landed in front of them.
They **will be studying** when you join them on Monday.

Perfect Continuous:
They **have been studying** together for five years.
They **had been studying** together for five minutes when a UFO **landed** in front of them.
They **will have been studying** for two hours when you join them on Monday.

Perfect:
They **have studied** together for five years.
They **had studied** flying instructions when a UFO landed in front of them.
They **will have studied** together for two hours when you join them.

Capitolo 8: Il segreto per usare i tempi verbali come un nativo

Curiosità:

Se leggiamo un libro, dopo due settimane, ne ricordiamo solo il 21%.

Piuttosto che imparare tonnellate di istruzioni, che vengono dimenticate dopo due settimane, impariamo i tempi attraverso gli esercizi. Per apprendere davvero i tempi inglesi, li fissiamo nella nostra mente subconscia e facciamo loro conoscenza automatica.

E congratulazioni - hai già iniziato a farlo!

Tuttavia, consultare questo libro solo una o due volte non è abbastanza. Otterrai un maggior successo nell'apprendimento se continuerai a ripetere gli esempi e gli esercizi in questo libro fino a quando non diventano conoscenza automatica.

Ricordi che imparare i tempi inglesi è come imparare a nuotare? Consultando questo libro una volta, sei caduto a capofitto nella piscina... ora devi usarlo per praticare le tue abilità di nuoto. Leggi gli esercizi di questo libro a voce alta, continuamente. Se hai la versione audio, ascolta e ripeti la registrazione molte volte. Una volta acquisite le informazioni nel tuo subconscio, i tempi inglesi diventeranno conoscenza automatica.

Note sull'autore

Ken Xiao

Ken è una fonte d'ispirazione per gli studenti di inglese. Ha imparato con successo a parlare inglese come un madrelingua in sei mesi usando una formula che aveva scoperto. È stato interprete del Dipartimento della Difesa degli Stati Uniti. Ora è un insegnante di inglese, preside scolastico e autore.

Urison Xiao

Urison pubblicò il suo primo libro quando aveva otto anni. Ama scrivere e scrive ogni giorno. Mentre il suo primo libro è un fumetto, il libro su cui sta lavorando al momento è un romanzo.

Altri libri di Ken Xiao

www.ingramcontent.com/pod-product-compliance
Lightning Source LLC
Chambersburg PA
CBHW031534040426
42445CB00010B/527